ideas

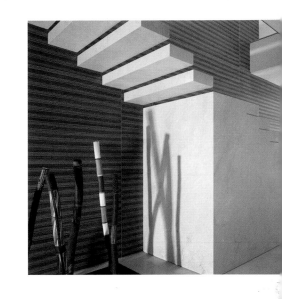

ideas

decoration
decoración
décoration
dekoration

AUTHORS
Fernando de Haro & Omar Fuentes

EDITORIAL DESIGN & PRODUCTION

ARQUITECTOS
EDITORES
MEXICANOS

PROJECT MANAGERS
Valeria Degregorio Vega
Tzacil Cervantes Ortega

COORDINATION
Susana Madrigal Gutiérrez
Adriana García Hernández

COPYWRITER
Roxana Villalobos

ENGLISH TRANSLATION
Louis Loizides

FRENCH TRANSLATION
Cécile Usselmann (Centro Profesional de Traducción e Interpretación / IFAL)

GERMAN TRANSLATION
Heike Ruttkowski

Ideas
decoration · decoración · décoration · dekoration

© 2007, Fernando de Haro & Omar Fuentes

AM Editores S.A. de C.V.
Paseo de Tamarindos 400 B, suite 102, Col. Bosques de las Lomas,
C.P. 05120, México, D.F. Tels. 52(55) 5258 0279, Fax. 52(55) 5258 0556.
E-mail: ame@ameditores.com   www.ameditores.com

ISBN 10: 970-9726-66-8
ISBN 13: 978-970-9726-66-4

Printed in China.

introduction   introducción

THE MOST INTENSELY PERSONAL THINGS anyone can have in the course of their life are their home and their clothing; both reflect the tastes, preferences, requirements and lifestyle of the person in question; but they are also an expression of their creativity and their relationship with the material world around them.

Home decoration is such a personal thing that it is almost impossible to talk about good or bad tastes: what for some might be very tasteful could equally

LO MÁS PERSONAL que un ser humano puede tener a lo largo de su vida es su hogar y su vestimenta; ambos son reflejo de sus gustos, preferencias, necesidades y de su modo de vivir; pero también expresan su creatividad y la forma en la que se relaciona con el mundo material que le circunda.

La decoración del hogar es algo tan individual que es prácticamente imposible hablar de buen o mal gusto, lo que en algún lado es visto como el mejor de los gustos en otro puede ser todo lo contrario. De modo

introduction   einleitung

DANS LA VIE, notre foyer et nos vêtements sont ce que nous avons de plus personnel ; c'est à ce niveau-là que nous pouvons exprimer nos goûts, nos préférences, nos besoins et notre mode de vie ainsi que notre créativité et notre rapport au monde qui nous entoure.

La décoration est quelque chose de tellement individuel qu'il est pratiquement impossible de parler de bon ou de mauvais goût ; ce que certains trouveront magnifique sera perçu par d'autres comme le comble de l'horreur et vice-versa. Chacun doit donc

DAS PERSÖNLICHSTE, was ein Mensch im Verlauf seines Lebens besitzen kann, sind seine Wohnung und seine Kleidung; beide spiegeln seinen Geschmack, seine Vorlieben, Bedürfnisse und seine Lebensart wider; sie drücken aber auch seine Kreativität und die Beziehung aus, die er zu der materielle Welt in seiner Umgebung hat.

Die Dekoration der Wohnung ist etwas so persönliches, dass es praktisch unmöglich ist von gutem oder schlechtem Geschmack zu sprechen. Was an einem Ort

be the opposite for others. The idea is therefore to create settings that are suitable and attractive for each person.

This book contains ideas obtained from the work of top interior designers, decorators and architects. They are not unique or absolute recipes or formulas to be followed to the letter, but simply concepts for readers to take the parts they need and devise their own decorative scheme.

This volume consists of six strategically-defined sections, covering most of the spaces and decorative elements of a home. It includes chapters on how to decorate living rooms, dining rooms, bathrooms, bedrooms and terraces, and an additional section has been included on decorative items of particular importance in interior design.

que de lo que se trata es de crear ambientes que le resulten adecuados y acogedores a cada uno.

Este libro contiene algunas ideas que han sido rescatadas del trabajo de los interioristas, decoradores y arquitectos más reconocidos. Si bien no se muestran recetas ni fórmulas únicas y definitivas, como si hubiera que seguirlas a manera de Biblia, sí se exponen conceptos para que cada quien tome de aquí y de allá y forme con su criterio su propia alternativa decorativa.

El volumen ha sido dividido de forma estratégica en seis secciones, abarcando la mayor parte de las áreas espaciales y elementos decorativos de una casa. Así, están contenidos los capítulos de decoración para salas, comedores, baños, recámaras y terrazas, y se ha añadido un apartado para hacer referencia a

se créer un espace sur mesure pour être certain de s'y sentir à son aise.

Ce livre contient un certain nombre d'idées empruntées à des décorateurs et à des architectes qui comptent parmi les plus renommés de la profession. Nous n'avons pas de recettes ou de formules magiques qu'il suffirait d'appliquer au pied de la lettre à vous proposer ; nous nous sommes donc contentés de vous présenter un certain nombre de concepts pour que vous puissez y piocher ci et là ce dont vous pourrez vous inspirer pour décorer votre chez-vous selon vos goûts personnels.

Ce volume a été divisé en six sections stratégiques ; nous avons ainsi consacré un chapitre à chaque pièce de la maison (salon, salle à manger, salle de bains, chambre à coucher et terrasse) et ajouté un

als sehr guter Geschmack wahrgenommen wird, kann an einem anderen Ort genau das Gegenteil bewirken. Daher geht es darum eine Atmosphäre zu schaffen, die für jeden einzelnen angemessen und angenehm ist.

Dieses Buch enthält einige Ideen, die von den bekanntesten Innendekorateuren, Dekorateuren und Architekten stammen. Es werden dabei keine Rezepte und auch keine einzigartigen oder endgültigen Formeln gegeben, die man zu befolgen hat als würde es sich um die Bibel handeln. Es werden vielmehr Konzepte vorgestellt, aus denen jeder einzelne aussucht was ihm gefällt. So kann gemäss dem individuellen Geschmack ein eigener, dekorativer Stil entwickelt werden.

Der Band wurde auf strategische Weise in sechs Abschnitte unterteilt, wobei die meisten Räume und dekorativen Elemente eines Hauses abgedeckt

Most of the ideas presented converge to generate an interesting eclecticism, without undermining the harmony that is essential for decoration. These pages also set out the versatility of materials available today, as well as the range of formal and design aspects afforded by furniture and fittings.

The solutions offered are equally diverse and plural; most are easy to achieve and will suit different budgets, as their greatest value lies in their contribution to improving quality of life, and their sole intention is to act as a catalyst to kick-start this process of transformation.

aquellos elementos decorativos que tienen un peso particular en el interiorismo.

La mayor parte de las ideas que se presentan convergen en un interesante eclecticismo, sin que por ello se caiga en la ruptura de la armonía siempre necesaria en la decoración. También se puede constatar a lo largo de las páginas la versatilidad de materiales con los que se cuenta hoy en día, así como la multiplicidad en cuanto a aspectos formales y de diseño de mobiliario y objetos.

Las soluciones que se muestran son igualmente diversas y plurales; la mayoría de ellas sencillas de lograr y fáciles de adecuar a distintos presupuestos para poder llevarlas a cabo, pues, en realidad, su mayor valor se encuentra en la aportación de conceptos que sirvan para lograr una mejor calidad de vida y sólamente tienen la pretensión de hacer las veces de combustible que ayude a que cada quien arranque su motor.

chapitre qui concerne les éléments qui jouent un rôle particulier dans la décoration intérieure.

La plupart des idées présentées ici constituent un éclectisme intéressant ; elles n'en respectent pas moins les règles de l'harmonie qui sont essentielles en matière de décoration. Vous pourrez également constater à la lecture de ces pages que nous avons tenté de rendre compte de la versatilité des matériaux actuels et de la multiplicité de formes et de styles que les objets et le mobilier peuvent adopter.

Les solutions que nous vous présentons ici sont diverses et plurielles ; la plupart d'entre elles sont simples à réaliser et s'adaptent au budget de chacun. Ces idées sont avant tout destinées à vous encourager à vous lancer dans la décoration et à prendre en main l'amélioration de votre cadre de vie, et c'est là que réside leur valeur principale.

werden. Es wird die Dekoration für Wohnzimmer, Esszimmer, Badezimmer, Schlafzimmer und Terrassen behandelt. Ferner wurde ein Abschnitt denjenigen dekorativen Elementen gewidment, die im Hinblick auf die Innendekoration von besonderer Bedeutung sind.

Die meisten der vorgestellten Ideen konvergieren in einem interessanten Eklektizismus, ohne dass dadurch die Harmonie gestört wird, die für die Dekoration stets unabdingbar ist. Auch wird auf den Seiten gezeigt, wie vielseitig die Materialien heutzutage sind; das gleiche gilt für die Formen und das Design von Möbeln und Objekten.

Die vorgestellten Lösungen sind genauso verschiedenartig wie vielfältig; die meisten Lösungen sind einfach zu verwirklichen und leicht an die unterschiedlichen, zur Verfügung stehenden Budgets anzugleichen. Im Grunde geht es darum Konzepte vorzustellen, die eine bessere Lebensqualität ermöglichen und Energie liefern, damit jeder einzelne in Schwung kommt.

living rooms
salas
salons
wohnzimmer

chimneys
chimeneas
cheminées
kamine

THE CHIMNEY is the main factor for defining a room as cozy. Its capacity for generating heat depends on the type, the one that creates the most being the traditional chimney, with the open fireplace, made with stone or brick sides and using firewood. The heat recuperator, which works using a metal box with a glass door, is ideal for regulating how much firewood is burned.

LA CHIMENEA es el elemento que mayormente permite calificar a un espacio como acogedor. Su capacidad calorífica depende de su tipo. La tradicional, con el hogar –espacio donde se enciende el fuego– abierto, formado por paredes de piedra o ladrillo en cuyo interior se quema la leña, ofrece bajo rendimiento calórico. La recuperadora de calor, que funciona a través de una caja metálica con puerta acristalada, es excelente para regular la combustión de los leños. La de gas brinda buenas posibilidades térmicas.

C'EST LA CHEMINEE qui apporte à une pièce son caractère chaleureux. Cela dit, toutes les cheminées n'ont pas les mêmes capacités de chauffage. Le modèle traditionnel, à foyer ouvert entouré de murs de pierre ou de brique, n'offre qu'un rendement limité. Le récupérateur de chaleur à caisson métallique et porte en verre permet en revanche de réguler au mieux la combustion des bûches. Les cheminées à gaz sont également très performantes au niveau thermique.

DER KAMIN ist ein Element, das dem Raum dazu verhilft wirklich gemütlich zu wirken. Die Wärmequalität hängt vom Typ des Kamins ab. Der traditionelle offene Kamin, in dessen Inneren bei offenem Feuer Holz verbrannt wird und der aus Stein- oder Ziegelwänden besteht, gibt wenig Hitze ab. Ein Kamin, der die Hitze zurückhält, innen mit Metall ausgestattet ist und eine gläserne Tür aufweist, ist hervorragend dazu geeignet, die Verbrennung des Holzes zu regulieren. Auch ein Gaskamin bietet gute thermische Eigenschaften.

THE LOCATION OF THE CHIMNEY can define the central axis around which the room is arranged. One option is to use it to generate two clearly differentiated areas, so, in addition to functioning as a divider, it will generate heat for both sides. If these spaces are the living room and the dining room, then it is a good idea to take care in choosing the shape and type of materials, as their visual impact is substantial and they will affect or define the overall decorative tone.

LA UBICACIÓN DE LA CHIMENEA puede servir para marcar el eje en torno al cual se organice el espacio. Una opción es aprovecharla, inclusive, para generar dos áreas claramente diferenciadas; de este modo, además de funcionar como muro divisorio, su poder calórico abarcará ambos lugares. Si se trata de la sala y el comedor es conveniente tener cuidado con la forma y el tipo de materiales por los que se opte, pues éstos tendrán un gran peso visual y afectarán o definirán la atmósfera decorativa general.

L'EMPLACEMENT DE LA CHEMINÉE peut servir de point de repère pour l'organisation du reste de l'espace. On peut d'ailleurs utiliser la cheminée comme paroi de séparation pour définir deux zones bien distinctes l'une de l'autre ; les deux sections recevront de plus la même quantité de chaleur. Si vous divisez votre pièce en salon et salle à manger, choisissez bien la forme et le type de matériaux car ils auront une présence visuelle non négligeable, ce qui peut affecter l'ensemble de la décoration et de l'atmosphère.

DER STANDORT DES KAMINES kann als Achse dienen, um die herum der Raum organisiert wird. Eine Möglichkeit ist die Nutzung des Kamins zur klaren Abgrenzung von zwei Bereichen. So dient er als Trennmauer und gleichzeitig auch als Wärmequelle für beide Bereiche. Wenn es sich dabei um Wohnzimmer und Esszimmer handelt, sollten die Form und das Material sorgfältig ausgewählt werden, denn der Kamin hat ein grosses optisches Gewicht und definiert oder beeinträchtigt die allgemeine dekorative Atmosphäre.

Chimneys come in all shapes and sizes. Floor to ceiling ones look good but can be heavy on the eye unless they are made with visually light materials. Medium-height chimneys are easier on the eye and their shaft can be esthetically arranged to blend in with the decoration.

Existen chimeneas con las más diversas formas y tamaños. Las de piso a techo son atractivas pero podrían ser pesadas si no son hechas con materiales que resulten visualmente ligeros; las de altura media son más livianas a la vista y su tiro puede resolverse estéticamente otorgando equilibrio a la decoración.

Il existe des cheminées de toutes formes et de toutes tailles. Celles allant du sol au plafond sont attrayantes, mais leur structure peut s'avérer lourde si elle n'est pas faite de matériaux visuellement légers ; celles montant à mi-hauteur sont plus sobres et l'estétique de leur hotte peut se travailler grâce à par une décoration équilibrée.

Offene Kamine können verschiedene Formen und Grössen aufweisen. Diejenigen, die vom Boden bis zur Decke reichen sind attraktiv anzusehen, können aber optisch schwer wirken, wenn sie nicht aus visuell leichten Materialien gefertigt sind. Mittelgrosse Kamine sind daher angebrachter, da sie eher mit der Dekoration im Einklag stehen.

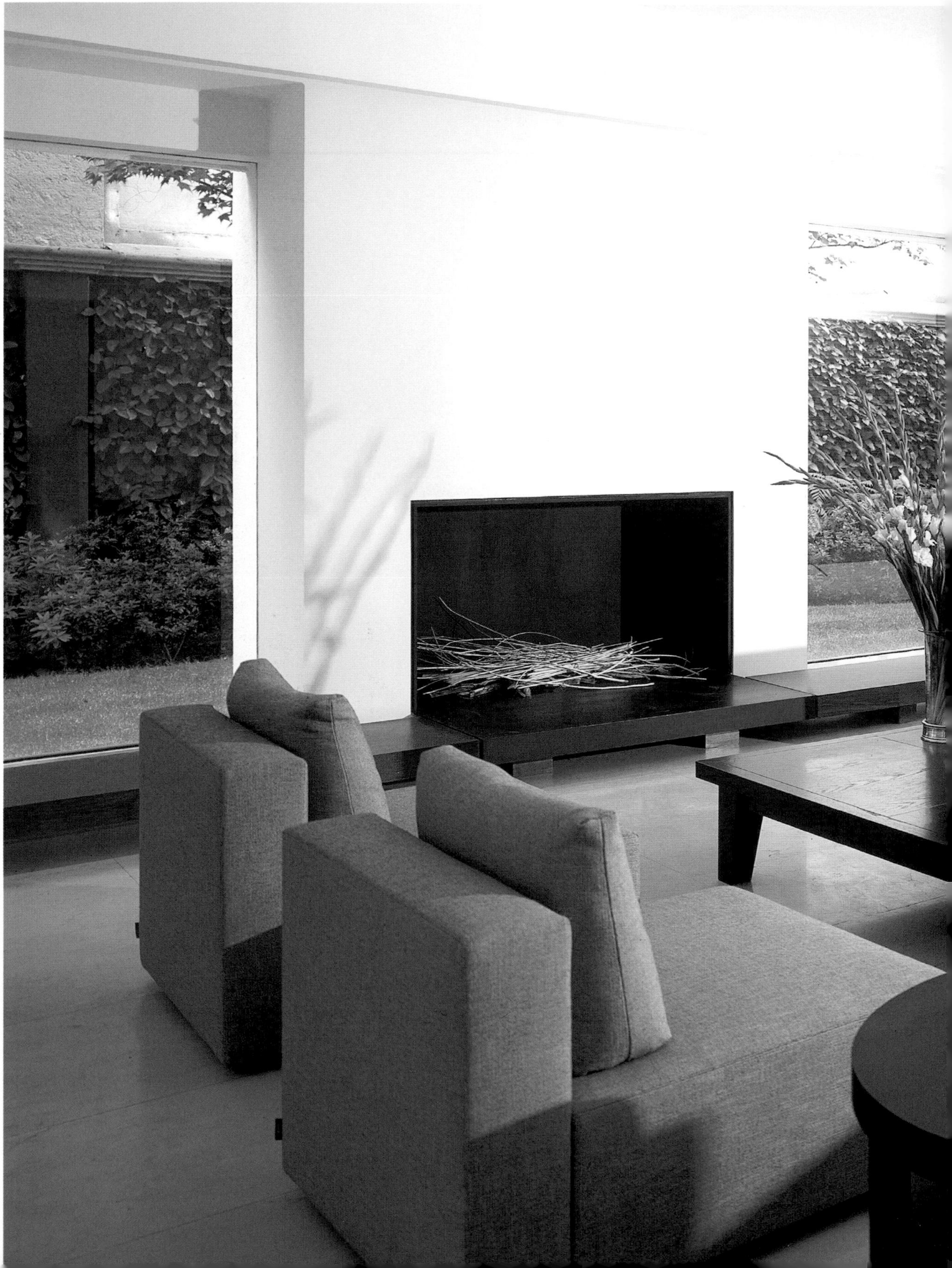

Chimneys in the Middle Ages were made from stone, then in the Seventeenth Century marble and wood became the common option, as did iron and porcelain in the Nineteenth Century. Today they are made from stone, marble and chromed metal, stainless steel, wood, shale and even mirrors; just about anything goes.

En la Edad Media dominaron las chimeneas de piedra, durante el siglo XVII las de mármol y madera, y durante el XIX las de hierro y las de porcelana. Hoy en día se hacen de piedra, mármol, metal cromado, acero inoxidable, madera, pizarra e incluso de espejo; y prácticamente cualquier material es válido.

Au Moyen-Âge, les cheminées étaient en pierre ; au XVII siècle, on passa au marbre et au bois pour en venir au fer et à la porcelaine au XIX siècle. À l'heure actuelle, il existe des cheminées en pierre, en marbre, en métal chromé, en acier inoxydable, en bois, en ardoise, voire même recouvertes de miroirs. Tous ces matériaux se valent et votre choix ne dépend que de vos goûts personnels.

Im Mittelalter wurden vorwiegend Steinkamine verwendet, im XVII. Jahrhundert Kamine aus Marmor und Holz und im XIX. Jahrhundert Eisen- und Porzellankamine. Heutzutage werden Kamine aus Stein, Marmor, verchromtem Metall, rostfreiem Stahl, Holz, Schiefer und sogar aus Spiegeln gefertigt. Praktisch jedes Material ist zulässig.

Iron is an excellent choice for making a large rustic chimney. Its size can be toned down with the use of wall paneling.

El hierro es una excelente opción para realizar una chimenea rústica y de grandes proporciones, su volumetría se puede disminuir usando lambrines.

Le fer est un matériau parfait si vous aimez le style rustique et les grandes cheminées ; pour atténuer l'aspect massif de votre cheminée, vous pouvez tapisser le mur de lambris.

Eisen ist eine hervorragende Alternative für einen rustikalen Kamin mit grossen Proportionen, dessen Volumetrie optisch verringert werden kann.

side and center tables
mesas de centro y laterales
tables basses
wohnzimmer- und beistelltische

THE TABLE IN THE MIDDLE OF THE LIVING ROOM, along with the decorative items on it, and the side tables are objects that complement the suite, but they are also ornamental articles with a significant presence and visual impact in this room, which means their presence plays a key role in the perception of space. This does not mean, however, that their original practical functions should be overlooked, as comfort depends largely on this.

SI BIEN LA MESA AL CENTRO DE LA SALA, los elementos decorativos que se colocan sobre ella y las mesas laterales son elementos complementarios del juego de sala, también son las partes de la decoración con mayor presencia y visualización en esta área, por lo que su presencia es determinante en la percepción del espacio. Sin embargo, no por ello hay que descuidar su función utilitaria original, pues de ésta dependen el confort y la comodidad.

LA TABLE BASSE PLACÉE AU CENTRE DU SALON, les objets décoratifs qu'on y pose et les tables d'angle doivent s'harmoniser avec vos canapés et fauteuils ; par leur présence visuelle, ces tables joueront un rôle déterminant sur la perception de l'espace. Pour les choisir, vous devrez donc tenir compte de leur aspect esthétique tout autant que de leur fonction utilitaire, essentielle pour votre confort.

DER WOHNZIMMERTISCH, die Dekoration, die darauf gestellt wird und die Beistelltische sind ergänzende Elemente des Wohnzimmers. Es handelt sich dabei auch um die Teile der Dekoration, die die grösste Aufmerksamkeit in diesem Bereich auf sich ziehen. Daher ist das Vorhandensein dieser Elemente wesentlich für die Wahrnehmung des Raumes. Dennoch ist die eigentliche praktische Funktion nicht zu vergessen, denn davon hängt der Komfort und die Bequemlichkeit ab.

A more clearly defined ambience can be created if there is harmony between the architectural items and furniture in a living room. It is therefore a good idea to ensure the larger objects match in terms of color, texture and shape. Accentuation can be achieved through accessories or details such as table bases or legs; surface finishes or moldings and edges. For instance, a 70s-style base with sinewy or organic shapes will provide a retro feel for a modern furniture arrangement.

Generar armonía entre los elementos arquitectónicos y el mobiliario de una sala cooperará a conseguir atmósferas definidas. De este modo, será útil conservar una unidad compositiva en las piezas grandes en cuanto a color, texturas y formas. El acento se puede lograr a través de los accesorios o detalles como son las bases de las mesas o sus patas; los acabados de sus superficies o bien sus molduras y cantos. Por ejemplo, una base de formas sinuosas u orgánicas, que recuerde los 70's, dará un toque retro a una composición con mobiliario moderno.

L'harmonie entre les éléments d'architecture et le mobilier du salon permet de créer une atmosphère bien précise. Il est préférable de conserver une certaine unité de couleur, de texture et de forme en ce qui concerne les meubles volumineux. La touche originale peut provenir des accessoires ou du choix en ce qui concerne le support, les pieds, les finitions et les formes des tables basses. Un support aux formes sinueuses ou organiques rappelant le style des années 70 apportera une touche rétro à un ensemble contemporain.

Wenn Harmonie zwischen den architektonischen Elementen und den Möbeln eines Wohnzimmers besteht, so trägt dies dazu bei, eine definierte Atmosphäre zu schaffen. Daher ist es angebracht, die grossen Teile im Hinblick auf deren Farbe, Textur und Formen aufeinander abzustimmen. Ein Akzent kann durch Accessoires oder Details gesetzt werden, wie zum Beispiel der Sockel des Tisches oder die Tischbeine, sowie auch das Material der Oberflächen, bzw. die Einfassungen und Kanten. So erinnert ein Sockel mit kurvigen oder einheitlichen Formen an die 70er Jahre. Ein solcher Tisch gibt einer Zusammenstellung aus modernen Möbeln einen nostalgischen Touch.

If the overall ambience is dominated by individual items of furniture such as stools and armchairs, a good idea would be to use square, straight-lined center tables that highlight the perimeters of the room. This effect can be enhanced by using contrasting colors for the floor and tables.

Si en el ambiente general predominan los muebles individuales como taburetes y sillones, conviene recurrir a mesas de centro cuadradas y de líneas rectas que remarquen los perímetros espaciales. Para reforzar el efecto es mejor usar colores contrastados entre los pisos y las mesas.

Si votre salon est surtout meublé de fauteuils, de tabourets ou de repose-pieds, les tables basses carrées et rectilignes vous conviendront mieux et permettront de définir le périmètre de l'espace. Pour améliorer cet effet, choisissez des tables d'une couleur radicalement différente de celles de vos sols.

Wenn im Allgemeinen im Raum einzelne Möbel, wie Sessel und Hocker überwiegen, sollten als Wohnzimmertisch quadratische Stücke ausgewählt werden, deren gerade Linien die räumlichen Umfänge hervorheben. Zur Verstärkung dieses Effektes sollte der Boden eine Farbe aufweisen, die in Kontrast zur Farbe des Tisches steht.

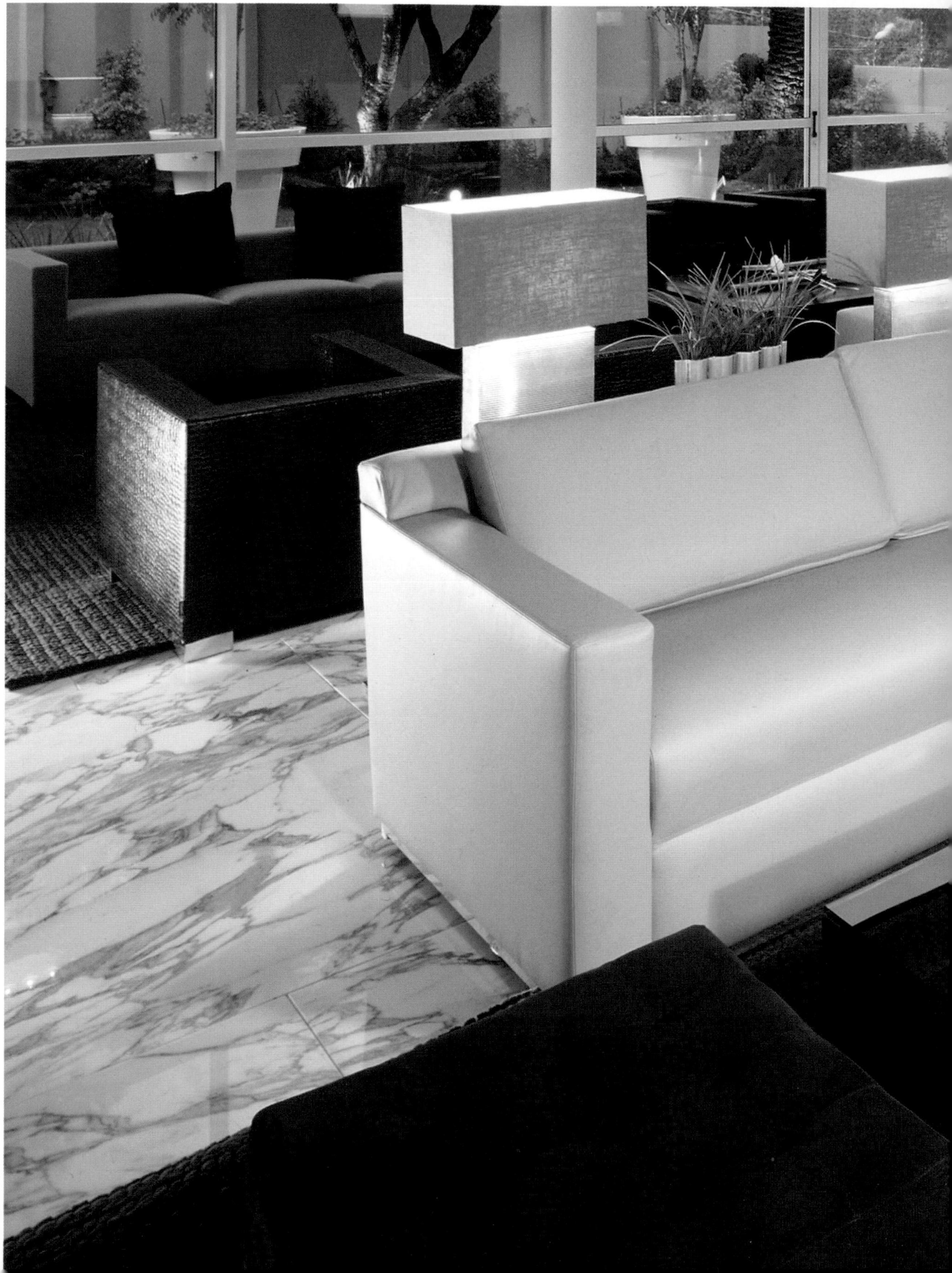

Center tables come in all sorts of shapes and sizes. The classic rectangular tables, whose esthetic quality is dominated by straight lines, are ideal for making the most of the length of the room and also combine well with elongated living room furniture where sofas prevail over individual armchairs. Their tops are shown without any ornamental motifs and are made from solid materials such as onyx, marble and planks of wood. Sometimes these solid materials can be combined with other lighter ones, such as glass.

Existe un gran espectro posible de formas y materiales para mesas de centro. Las clásicas mesas rectangulares, en cuya estética general domina la línea recta, facilitan el aprovechamiento longitudinal del espacio y resultan muy apropiadas para muebles de sala con proporciones alargadas en donde dominan los sofás sobre los sillones individuales. Sus tableros se presentan ausentes de motivos ornamentales y se hacen en materiales sólidos como el ónix, el mármol y la madera en tablón; o a veces combinan materiales macizos con otros ligeros como el vidrio.

Il existe un spectre infini de formes et de matériaux en matière de tables basses. Les tables rectangulaires classiques et rectilignes permettent de tirer parti de l'espace longitudinal et sont tout à fait appropriées quand on possède des meubles de salon aux proportions allongées, quand les canapés, et non les fauteuils, dominent l'espace. Les tables basses de ce type possèdent un plateau lisse et sans ornements ; les matériaux de choix seront l'onyx, le marbre et le bois massif. Vous pouvez aussi choisir un support massif sur lequel vous poserez une plaque de verre.

Es sind viele Formen und Materialien für Wohnzimmertische vorhanden. Die klassischen rechteckigen Tische, deren Ästhetik sich auf gerade Linien stützt, helfen bei der längsausgerichteten Nutzung des Raumes. Sie sind besonders geeignet für Wohnzimmermöbel mit langen Porportionen, bei denen mehr Sofas als einzelne Sessel zum Einsatz kommen. Die Tischplatten weisen keine Verzierungen auf und werden aus soliden Materialien, wie Onyx, Marmor oder Holz gefertigt. Eine weitere Alternative ist die Kombination von massiven Materialien mit leichten Materialien, wie zum Beispiel Glas.

One design option for center tables is to join several small tables together, including nest tables placed one inside the other, and which can be put together in different ways. The decoration acquires great mobility if they are placed in a cross-sectional manner.

Dentro del diseño de mesas de centro se halla la opción de varias mesillas que se puedan empalmar, incluyendo las de nido que se meten unas dentro de otras y permiten ser colocadas de distintas maneras. Cuando se les acomoda transversalmente la decoración adquiere gran movimiento.

Votre choix en matière de tables basses peut se porter sur les tables gigognes que vous pouvez ranger les unes sous les autres ou disposer de différentes manières selon vos besoins du moment. Disposées de façon transversale, elles apporteront mouvement et dynamisme à la décoration du salon.

Im Rahmen des Designs von Wohnzimmertischen können auch mehrere Tische gewählt werden, die zusammen eine Einheit bilden. Es kann dabei eine Art Nest geformt werden, wobei Tische unter andere geschoben und auf verschiedene Art und Weise aufgestellt werden können. Werden sie quer angeordnet, sieht die Dekoration sehr bewegt aus.

Coastal regions offer an extensive range of materials, but they must be damp-resistant.

Las zonas de playa se prestan para utilizar una amplia gama de materiales, pero hay cuidar que éstos sean resistentes a la humedad.

En bord de mer, on peut utiliser une vaste gamme de matériaux à condition de veiller à ce qu'ils soient résistants à l'humidité.

Im Strandbereich können verschiedenartige Materialien verwendet werden. Dabei ist darauf zu achten, dass sie widerstandsfähig gegen Feuchtigkeit sind.

There is currently a broad range of original ideas for the design of center tables, including a single block with a powerful presence in the space or different units joined together to make a functional item of furniture. Whatever you choose, the size of these items must be balanced with the other furniture. One good way to do this is to align the tables so they run lengthwise with the armchairs and, especially, the sofa.

En la actualidad se cuenta con una amplia variedad de propuestas originales para el diseño de mesas de centro, incluyendo la alternativa de un bloque único que se signifique por su fuerte presencia dentro del espacio o a diversos módulos que unidos conformen un mueble funcional. Sea cual sea la elección, se debe equilibrar la masividad de los volúmenes con respecto al resto de los muebles. Para conseguirlo, es aconsejable colocar las mesas de modo que recorran las superficies longitudinales de los sillones y especialmente las del sofá.

Il existe à l'heure actuelle une grande variété de designs originaux en matière de tables basses ; vous pouvez par exemple choisir un bloc massif qui aura une forte présence dans l'espace ou au contraire différents modules dont l'ensemble formera un meuble fonctionnel. Quel que soit votre choix, tentez d'obtenir un équilibre entre le volume de la table et celui des autres meubles. Pour y parvenir, nous vous conseillons d'aligner la table sur le côté le plus long du canapé.

Derzeit gibt es eine grosse Vielfalt an originellen Ideen für das Design von Wohnzimmertischen. Dabei kann ein einziger, dominanter Sockel gewählt werden oder verschiedene Module, die zusammen ein zweckmässiges Möbel bilden. Gleichgültig welche Alternative gewählt wird, sollte das Volumen im Hinblick auf den Rest der Möbel stets ausgewogen sein. In diesem Zusammenhang ist es ratsam die Tische so aufzustellen, dass sie längs zu den Sesseln und besonders auch zum Sofa stehen.

sofas and stools
sofás, sillones y taburetes
canapés et tabourets
sofas und sessel

SOFAS, ARMCHAIRS AND STOOLS must be both comfortable and functional, made to create a space to be shared harmoniously or for relaxation. The way these items are distributed will define how people rest in or share the living room. Options range from the planning of a single armchair to arranging the room in an "L" or "U" shape, as well as positioning sofas and armchairs so they face each other.

SOFÁS, SILLONES Y TABURETES deben ser muebles cómodos y funcionales, concebidos para generar espacios en donde se lleve a cabo una convivencia confortable o que sirvan para el relajamiento. La manera en que se distribuyen define el modo en que se llevará a cabo la reunión o el descanso en una sala. Por ello, es posible planear desde un sillón aislado, hasta la disposición de una sala en forma de "L" o de "U", o la ubicación de sofás y sillones enfrentados.

LES CANAPES, LES FAUTEUILS ET LES TABOURETS doivent être confortables et fonctionnels ; ils doivent de plus vous permettre d'aménager votre espace de manière à favoriser la conversation et la détente. La façon dont vous les disposerez définira l'ambiance qui règnera dans votre salon. Vous pouvez ainsi choisir entre différents aménagements possibles : un fauteuil isolé dans un coin, un ensemble canapé en forme de "L" ou de "U", deux canapés disposés en face l'un de l'autre.

SOFAS, SESSEL UND HOCKER sollten bequem und zweckmässig sein und dazu dienen einen Raum zu schaffen, der ein behagliches und entspanntes Zusammenleben ermöglicht. Die Aufstellung der Möbel definiert die Art und Weise, wie ein Treffen oder die Erholung im Wohnzimmer ablaufen. Daher kann sowohl ein einzelner Sessel aufgestellt werden oder die Couchgarnitur in L- oder U-Form disponiert werden. Als weitere Alternative können die Sofas gegenüber der Sessel aufgestellt werden.

The combination of wood and upholstery textures plays a vital role in the conception and sensuality of space.

La combinación de maderas con las texturas de las tapicerías adquiere una enorme importancia en la concepción del espacio y su sensualidad.

La combinaison habile du bois et des tissus joue un rôle vital dans la conception et la sensualité de l'espace.

Die Kombination von Holz mit den Texturen der Polster ist sehr wichtig für die Wahrnehmung des Raumens und dessen Sinnlichkeit.

If you prefer to lighten the ambience and lessen the presence of the sofas, one good option is to use two armchairs as a complement for the living room and for them to break away from the other furniture, standing out for their color and finishes.

Cuando se desea aligerar el ambiente y restar peso a los sofás es recomendable el uso de dos sillones como complemento de la sala, mismos que conviene que rompan formalmente con los otros muebles y se distingan de ellos por su color y acabados.

Pour contrebalancer le poids visuel d'un canapé volumineux, vous pouvez disposer deux fauteuils qui se distingueront du reste du mobilier de par leurs formes et leurs coloris.

Soll die Atmosphäre leicht und das optische Gewicht der Sofas gering sein, ist es empfehlenswert zwei Sessel zu verwenden, die die Wohnzimmergarnitur vervollständigen. Diese Sessel sollten dabei eine andere Form als die übrigen Möbel aufweisen und sich auch durch Farbe und Material abheben.

One option for creating a clean and serene setting consists of using pure, straight-lined furniture with light-colored upholstery free of any designs, and positioning it so that it follows the natural perimeters of the walls. Paintings and items placed on the table will afford some warmth, as will the use of cushions, or even individual armchairs, with accentuated colors. Both effects can be enhanced by using a natural fiber rug to delimit the space and envelope the furniture.

Una alternativa para crear un ambiente muy limpio y sereno es, además de incluir mobiliario de líneas rectas, puras, tapizado en colores claros y sin estampado, acomodarlo siguiendo el perímetro natural de los muros. El toque de calidez se puede conseguir a través de cuadros o de los objetos que se coloquen sobre las mesas, poniendo un acento de color en los cojines e incluso en los sillones sueltos. Ambos efectos se pueden acrecentar si se opta por un tapete de fibra natural que delimite el espacio y circunde a los muebles.

Si vous souhaitez créer une ambiance sereine dans une pièce nette et bien rangée, nous vous conseillons de choisir des meubles aux lignes pures, recouverts de tissus unis et clairs, et de les disposer le long des murs. Les tableaux et les objets que vous poserez sur les tables apporteront une touche de couleur et de gaieté accentuée par la présence de coussins ou de fauteuils différents du reste du mobilier. Un tapis en fibre naturelle vous permettra de délimiter l'espace et de souligner à la fois la pureté des lignes de vos meubles et les touches de couleur que vous aurez apporté à l'ensemble.

Zur Schaffung einer sehr sauberen und ruhigen Atmosphäre, sollten die Möbel gerade und klare Linien aufweisen. Für die Polster sind helle Stoffe ohne Muster zu bevorzugen. Bei der Aufstellung der Möbel sollte dem Umriss der Wände gefolgt werden. Ein warmer Touch kann durch Bilder oder Objekte erzielt werden, die auf die Tische gestellt werden. Die Couchkissen können durch ihre Farbe einen Akzent setzen und sogar lose auf dem Sofa verteilt werden. Beide Effekte werden noch verstärkt, wenn ein Teppich aus Naturfasern gewählt wird, der den Bereich abgrenzt und die Möbel umgibt.

The advantage of beach furniture is that it makes the most of available space and is very comfortable; it often consists of embedded structures made from building materials on which cushions are placed to provide the seat and backrest. The upholstery is essential for both its appearance and its practicality, often made from thick, tough materials, and there is usually a zip or buttons so the cases can be taken off and washed. Because of this, if this option is chosen, there is no reason to see color as a limitation in decoration.

Los muebles de playa deben tener la ventaja de hacer rendir el espacio y ser muy cómodos; generalmente consisten en estructuras empotradas hechas de materiales constructivos sobre las que se colocan los cojines que conforman respaldos y asientos. La tapicería de estos últimos es fundamental tanto para la estética como para la funcionalidad, comúnmente se usan telas gruesas y resistentes, y se incluye un cierre que permita desfundarlas y lavarlas. Por esta razón, si se elige esta alternativa no es necesario pensar en el color como un factor limitante dentro de la decoración.

Les meubles de plage ont l'avantage d'être confortables et de permettre de tirer parti de l'espace. Ce sont généralement des structures permanentes, fabriquées en matériaux de construction, sur lesquels on pose des matelas ou des coussins. Le tissu de recouvrement est fondamental aussi bien en ce qui concerne l'effet esthétique que la fonctionnalité ; on préférera généralement les housses en tissu épais, résistant et lavable, munies de fermetures-éclair. Ce choix vous permet en plus de changer de coloris dès que vous le souhaitez.

Strandmöbel haben den Vorteil, dass der Raum grosszügig aussieht und sie sehr bequem sind. Normalerweise handelt es sich um feststehende Strukturen aus Baumaterialien, auf denen die Kissen angebracht werden, die als Lehne und Sitz dienen. Die Polster sind entscheidend für die Ästhetik und Zweckmässigkeit dieser Möbel. Im Allgemeinen werden grobe und widerstandsfähige Stoffe verwendet, die einen Reissverschluss aufweisen und so abgezogen und gewaschen werden können. Aus diesem Grunde ist bei dieser Alternative die Farbe nicht als ein einschränkender Faktor im Rahmen der Dekoration anzusehen.

dining rooms
comedores
salles à manger
esszimmer

DINING ROOM FURNITURE must strike a balance between its esthetic and functional roles, and satisfy specific usage requirements. The best way to furnish this room is by bearing in mind the size and shape of the space available. In other words, a rectangular or circular table will go better in a space of the same shape. This means it will ultimately be the contours of the dining room that define the type of table to use.

LAS PIEZAS DEL COMEDOR deben representar una síntesis entre estética y funcionalidad, y estar de acuerdo con las necesidades de uso particulares. Para amueblar este sitio lo más adecuado es basarse en las dimensiones y formas espaciales con las que se cuente. Es decir, una mesa rectangular o una circular se insertarán mejor en un espacio con su misma forma. De esta manera, será el propio perímetro del lugar el que defina el tipo de mesa a seleccionar.

LES ÉLÉMENTS DE LA SALLE À MANGER doivent être à fois fonctionnels, agréables à regarder et adaptés à nos besoins. Pour choisir vos meubles, le mieux est de vous inspirer des dimensions et de la structure de l'espace dont vous disposez. Ainsi, une table rectangulaire s'adaptera mieux à un espace de mêmes caractéristiques qu'une table ronde et viceversa. C'est donc le périmètre de la pièce qui va vous indiquer quel genre de table vous devez choisir.

DER ESSTISCH SOLLTE eine Synthese aus Ästhetik und Zweckmässigkeit darstellen und die speziellen Bedürfnisse decken. Zum Möblieren des Esszimmers ist es angebracht, sich auf die vorhandenen Ausmasse zu stützen. Das heisst, ein rechteckiger Tisch oder ein runder Tisch passen besser in einen Raum mit derselben Form. Daher ist es das Ausmass des Ortes, das die Art des Tisches bestimmt, den es auszuwählen gilt.

tables
mesas
tables
tische

Rectangular tables need more space than round ones because of their size and shape, but they allow for a "French style" arrangement, by which the host and main guest can sit at either end, thereby facilitating the positioning of the other hosts and guests.

Aunque por su dimensión y forma requieren de mayor espacio físico que las redondas, las mesas rectangulares permiten la ubicación "a la francesa", en la que el anfitrión y el invitado principal ocupan las cabeceras, facilitando con dicha disposición la del resto de los anfitriones e invitados.

De par leurs dimensions et leur forme, les tables rectangulaires prennent plus de place que les tables rondes ; en revanche, elle permettent de s'asseoir « à la française », autrement dit de placer l'hôte et son invité principal de part et d'autre de la table, tandis que les autres convives prennent place sur les côtés.

Obwohl rechteckige Tische aufgrund ihres Ausmasses und ihrer Form mehr Platz benötigen als runde Tische, haben sie dennoch den Vorteil, dass eine "französische" Sitzordnung möglich ist, bei der der Gastgeber und der wichtigste Gast vor Kopf sitzen. Ausgehend von dieser Anordnung kann dann die restliche Sitzordnung geplant werden.

If you want a sober ambience in the dining room, then you need simple, straight-lined furniture that is not too bulky. The brown tones of the wood can really stand out if the upholstery and coverings of the seats are based on light colors. On the other hand, if the latter are also dark brown, then some contrast should be provided by the floors and walls by using more brightly-colored wood for the former and darker colors for the latter. Paintings can add a touch of color to liven up the room.

Si lo que se desea es un estilo sobrio en el comedor es necesario optar por muebles de líneas rectas, simples y poco abultados. El color chocolate en las maderas es de gran impacto cuando las sillas son tapizadas y vestidas en tonos claros. En cambio, si estas últimas mantienen también el color chocolate, es recomendable crear contraste con los pisos y los muros usando una madera más clara en los primeros y colores claros en los segundos. El toque de color se puede lograr con cuadros que aviven el espacio.

Si vous préférez les ambiances sobres, choisissez des meubles rectilignes, simples et sans ornements. Des chaises en bois couleur chocolat au siège tapissé d'écru seront du plus bel effet. Veillez toutefois à créer un certain contraste entre les meubles, les parquets et les murs en choisissant des tons plus clairs pour ces derniers. Un tableau complètera l'ensemble et apportera une touche de couleur.

Soll das Esszimmer nüchtern wirken, müssen Möbel mit klaren und einfachen Linien ausgewählt werden, die nur wenig gewölbt sind. Braune Holztöne sehen gewaltig aus, wenn die Stühle mit hellem Stoff gepolstert sind. Wenn die Stühle jedoch auch in braun gehalten sind, ist es empfehlenswert den Boden und die Wände von dieser Farbe abzuheben. Dies kann durch helles Holz für den Boden und helle Farben an den Wänden erreicht werden. Ein farbiger Touch kann durch Gemälde erzielt werden, die den Raum lebendiger machen.

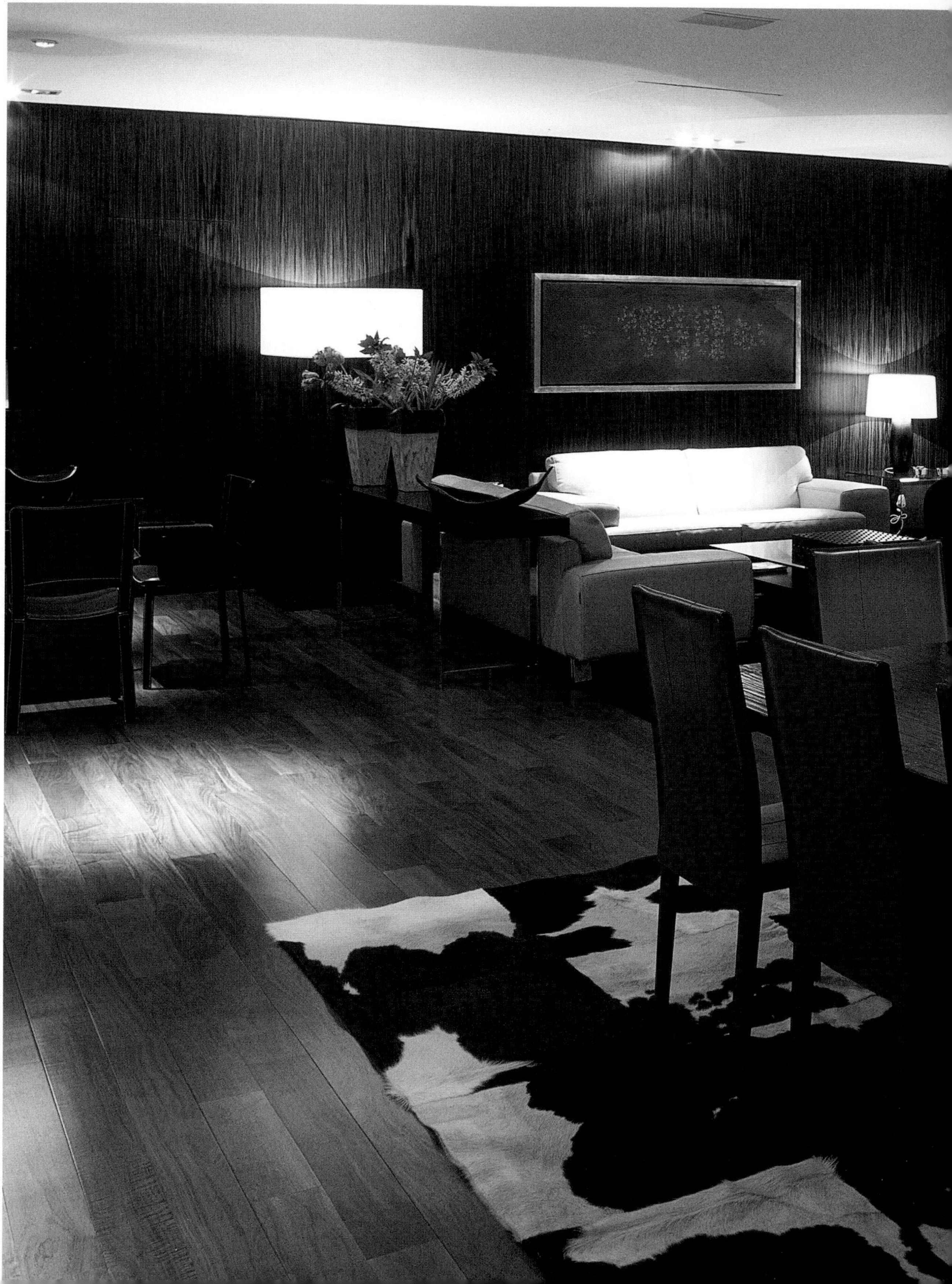

If the dining room and living room are not physically separate spaces, whatever happens in one will affect the other. The visual lightness of glass as the centerpiece of the decoration and its neutrality make it ideal for both areas and for generating harmony. Polished glass tables highlight the lightness of the volumes and enhance the quadrangular shapes. If, in addition, the presence of color is kept to a minimum, the expression of beauty in the space will be toned down.

Cuando la sala y el comedor no son dos sitios divididos espacialmente, lo que ocurre en un lado afecta al otro. La ligereza visual del cristal como eje de la decoración, así como su neutralidad, lo convierten en un material idóneo para usarse en ambas zonas y generar empatía. Las mesas de cristal esmerilado fortalecen la sensación de liviandad de los volúmenes y hacen resaltar las formas cuadrangulares. Si a ello se le suma la prácticamente nula presencia del color, la belleza del espacio es percibida en su mínima expresión.

Lorsque le salon et la salle à manger ne forment qu'une seule pièce, il est évident que chaque espace aura une incidence sur le second. Le verre étant un matériau neutre et de peu de présence visuelle, il peut être utilisé dans les deux espaces pour créer une certaine unité. Les tables en verre dépoli accentuent la légèreté des volumes et font ressortir les formes quadrangulaires. En supprimant les couleurs, vous obtiendrez un décor minimaliste de toute beauté.

Wenn das Wohnzimmer und das Esszimmer nicht räumlich getrennt sind, beeinflusst der eine Bereich den anderen. Die optische Leichtigkeit von Glas als Achse der Dekoration und deren Neutralität, machen daraus ein geeignetes Material, um in beiden Zonen verwendet zu werden und Harmonie zu schaffen. Tische aus geschliffenem Glas begünstigen die Leichtigkeit der Volumen und heben quadratische Formen hervor. Wenn dann noch in Betracht gezogen wird, dass praktisch keine Farbe verwendet wird, so wird auf einfach Weise ein attraktiver Raum geschaffen.

It is always interesting to combine materials in a single piece of furniture. Glass combined with metal, such as stainless steel, in a very linear table next to a wooden wall will create an attractive interplay between tradition and modernity.

La mezcla de materiales en un solo mueble es siempre interesante. El cristal combinado con metales del tipo del acero inoxidable en una mesa muy lineal que se encuentra junto a un muro rústico evocará la sensación de diálogo entre tradición y modernidad.

Un meuble fabriqué à partir de matériaux différents est toujours intéressant à regarder. Une plaque de verre sur support en acier inoxydable, placée contre un mur rustique, évoquera l'idée du dialogue entre tradition et modernité.

Verschiedene Materialien an einem einzigen Möbel wirken immer interessant. Glas mit Metall vom Typ rostfreier Edelstahl vereint an einem Tisch mit klaren Linien, der neben einer rustikalen Wand steht: diese Kombination ruft den Eindruck von Dialog zwischen Tradition und Modernität hervor.

Glass topped tables extend the space visually, as well as create reflections and contrasts with the light. Glass transparency options are numerous, and glass plates are also available in a broad range of thicknesses. Furthermore, the variety of finishes is extensive; the latter range from unpolished or treated glass, which is semi-translucent, to totally transparent flat glass. Before making a decision, it is best to analyze the space along with the elements and materials to be used.

Las mesas con cubiertas de cristal amplían visualmente el espacio y al contacto con la luz crean reflejos y contrastes. Sin embargo, las opciones de transparencia del vidrio son múltiples, los grosores en que se presentan sus láminas son de un amplio rango y los acabados son muy variables; estos últimos pueden ir desde el despulido o el cristal al ácido que son semi-translúcidos, hasta el vidrio plano totalmente transparente. Es aconsejable que la decisión provenga del análisis del espacio y de los elementos y materiales que conforman el conjunto.

Les tables en verre semblent occuper moins de place ; au contact du verre, la lumière crée des reflets et des contrastes agréables. La transparence du verre peut varier tout comme l'épaisseur des plaques. On trouve ainsi des plaques semi translucides en verre dépoli ou traité à l'acide ou des plaques totalement transparentes. Votre choix dépendra d'une analyse de l'espace et des autres matériaux que vous emploierez.

Tische mit Tischplatten aus Glas vergrössern den Raum optisch und bei Kontakt mit Licht, entstehen Reflexe und Kontraste. Die Durchsichtigkeit des Glases kann dabei unterschiedlich sein, so wie auch die Dicke der Platte und deren Oberfläche. Die Tischplatte kann sowohl geschliffen als auch geätzt sein, wobei ein halbdurchsichtiger Effekt entsteht. Eine andere Möglichkeit ist ein komplett durchsichtiges Glas. Es ist ratsam, die Entscheidung auf der Grundlage einer Analyse des Raumes sowie der darin vorhandenen Elemente und Materialien zu treffen.

Experimenting with the colors, tones and textures of the walls and tables will offer design options for achieving high impact visual effects.

Jugar tanto con los colores y sus tonalidades como con las texturas de los muros de remate y los de la mesa del comedor es una alternativa de diseño con la cual, sin lugar a dudas, se conseguirá un efecto de alto impacto visual.

En jouant avec les couleurs, les tons et les textures des murs et ceux de la table de la salle à manger, vous obtiendrez un effet saisissant.

Wird mit Farben, Farbtönen sowie mit Texturen der Wände und des Esstisches gespielt, wird ein Design erzielt, dass ohne Zweifel von besonderer optischer Attraktivität ist.

Tables with tops made from polished stone and wooden bases are very elegant. Stone seen edge-on will always highlight the exquisiteness and fineness of the furniture.

Resultan especialmente elegantes aquellas mesas cuyas superficies son de piedra pulida y son combinadas con bases de madera. Los cantos perfilados reafirman siempre la exquisitez y el delicado trabajo del mueble.

Une table en pierre polie ou composée d'une plaque en pierre posée sur un support en bois apportera immédiatement une touche d'élégance et de sophistication à votre salle à manger. Chaque coin ou bord de la table atteste du travail exquis de la pierre.

Besonders elegant wirken diejenigen Tische, deren Oberfläche aus poliertem Stein gefertigt ist und mit Tischbeinen aus Holz kombiniert wird. Die abgerundeten Kanten bestätigen die Erlesenheit und Feinheit des Möbels.

If a table is chosen because of the appeal of its shape, texture, materials and finishes, then it will afford personality to the space and play a leading decorative role. If it has relieves, they must be allowed to stand out by not placing any competing objects on them.

Si se selecciona una mesa llamativa por su forma, textura, materialidad y acabados, será ésta la que le otorgará personalidad al espacio y se convertirá en el objeto decorativo. Cuando cuenta con relieves hay que dejarlos lucir y no colocar encima objetos que les compitan.

Si vous choisissez une table impressionnante de par sa forme, sa texture, ses matériaux ou ses finitions, elle imposera sa personnalité au restant de la pièce et se transformera en objet décoratif. Évitez de placer sur la table des objets qui pourraient lui faire concurrence au niveau esthétique.

Wird ein Tisch gewählt, der eine auffällige Form, Textur, Material und Oberfläche aufweist, so trägt dies zur Persönlichkeit des Raumes bei und der Tisch verwandelt sich in ein dekoratives Objekt. Sind reliefartige Verzierungen vorhanden, sind diese hervorzuheben und keine Objekte auf den Tisch zu stellen, die die Aufmerksamkeit ablenken.

DINING ROOM CHAIRS must be comfortable; their armrests must be at the right height and very linear in order not to overload the chair, while their absence enhances the perception of lightness. It is good idea to make sure the number of chairs is proportional to the length of the table, as well as the size of the space they stand in. Their distribution will determine how comfortable the diners are, as will their backrests; if the backrests are high, they will support the whole of the back and be comfortable.

chairs
sillas
chaises
stühle

LA SILLA DEL COMEDOR debe ser cómoda; sus brazos tienen que conservar la altura apropiada y ser muy lineales para no recargar al mueble; si no cuentan con ellos la percepción es de mayor ligereza. Es recomendable que el número de asientos sea proporcional al largo o al diámetro de la mesa, así como al espacio en el que se ubiquen. De su distribución dependerá el confort de los comensales, tanto como de los respaldos que posean; cuando estos últimos son altos permiten el apoyo total de la espalda y son confortables.

LES CHAISES DE LA SALLE À MANGER doivent être confortables ; si vous choisissez des fauteuils, veillez à ce que les bras soient placés à la bonne hauteur sans ornemets pour ne pas surcharger l'aspect du meuble. Les chaises sont moins imposantes au niveau visuel que les fauteuils. Disposez un nombre de chaises proportionnel à la longueur ou au diamètre de la table et aux dimensions de la salle à manger. Le confort des convives dépendra de l'organisation des chaises autour de la table ainsi que de leur dossier. Les chaises à haut dossier soutiennent mieux le dos et sont donc plus confortables.

DIE ESSZIMMERTISCHSTÜHLE sollten bequem sein; die Armlehnen sollten eine geeignete Höhe aufweisen und länglich sein, damit sie nicht gegen die Möbel stossen. Sind keine Armlehnen vorhanden, trägt dies zur optischen Leichtigkeit bei. Es ist empfehlenswert, dass die Anzahl der Stühle proportional zu der Länge oder dem Durchmesser des Tisches sowie zum vorhandenen Platz gewählt wird. Von der Verteilung der Stühle sowie deren Rückenlehen hängt der Komfort der Tischgäste ab. Sind die Rückenlehnen hoch, so wird der Rücken vollständig abgestützt und daher sind diese Art von Stühlen besonders bequem.

If curved chairs are designed in accordance with ergonomic standards, their very curvature will become a kind of cozy "shell" ideal for resting the body. If the shapes of the seats are in harmony with those of the table, the effect will be enhanced.

Si las sillas de formas curvas están diseñadas de acuerdo con estándares ergonómicos, su propia curvatura se convertirá en una especie de "concha" acogedora en la que el cuerpo encontrará descanso. Cuando las formas de la silla se coordinan con las de la mesa la sensación es aún mejor.

Certaines chaises aux formes courbes sont conçues pour être ergonomiques ; leur forme crée alors une espèce de coquille dans laquelle on peut se lover. La sensation sera encore plus agréable si les chaises et la table forment un ensemble cohérent.

Wenn gewölbte Stühle in Übereinstimmung mit ergonomischen Normen designed wurden, verwandelt sich die Wölbung selbst in eine Art gemütliche "Muschel", in der der Körper zur Ruhe kommen kann. Werden die Formen der Stühle mit denen des Tisches in Einklang gebracht, so ist dieser Eindruck noch stärker.

Fully upholstered armchairs and chairs require very tough material. Brightly-colored material will mask the bulkiness of the furniture and make it look more stylish. Another option for achieving this effect is to combine wood with plain cloths.

Los sillones y las sillas que se encuentran tapizados en su totalidad deben utilizar telas muy resistentes. Los tapices claros disimulan el volumen del mueble y lo hacen ver más estilizado. Otra alternativa para restarle peso al mobiliario es combinar madera con telas lisas.

Si vous choisissez des fauteuils et des chaises tapissés, veillez à choisir un tissu d'ameublement très résistant. Les tissus clairs tendent à mieux définir les volumes tout en amenuisant leur présence. Les meubles en bois recouverts de tissus unis sont plus discrets.

Sessel und Stühle, die komplett gepolstert sind, sollten mit sehr widerstandsfähigen Stoffen bezogen werden. Helle Polster verbergen das Volumen des Möbels und erwecken einen gestylten Eindruck. Eine weitere Alternative, um den Möbeln weniger Gewicht zu geben, ist die Kombination von Holz mit Stoffen ohne Muster.

Round tables accommodate a greater number of seats and are ideal for a get-together, but it is advisable to make sure their supports do not get in the way of seating and people.

Las mesas redondas permiten acomodar un mayor número de sillas y favorecen la convivencia, pero hay que prever que sus apoyos no estorben al acomodo de las sillas y la gente.

Les tables rondes permettent de recevoir un plus grand nombre de personnes et favorisent la convivialité. Le support ou les pieds de la table ne doivent cependant pas gêner vos invités.

An runden Tischen können mehr Stühle untergebracht werden und dies begünstigt das Zusammenleben. Dabei ist darauf zu achten, dass die Lehnen nicht die Aufstellung der Stühle sowie die Personen behindern.

Leather is a good option for chair upholstery, providing both comfort and elegance, and adapts to ambient temperatures without getting hot or cold.

Las sillas de piel son una buena elección como tapicería; ofrecen la sensación de confort y elegancia, y el material se adapta a la temperatura ambiente sin ser frío ni caluroso.

Le cuir convient parfaitement pour tapisser vos chaises. C'est un matériau élégant et confortable qui s'adapte à la température ambiante sans jamais être ni trop chaud ni trop froid.

Lederstühle sind eine gute Wahl, denn sie bieten den Eindruck von Komfort und Eleganz und das Material passt sich an die Umgebungstemperatur an, ohne kalt oder warm zu sein.

An alternative to modern designs for furnishing a beach house involves fusing tradition and comfort. Esthetic designs in relief on the backrests of dining room chairs should be combined with comfortable seats and wide armrests.

Alejarse de los diseños modernos para amueblar una casa de playa invita a pensar en la fusión de tradición y confort. Los estéticos labrados en relieve sobre los respaldos de las sillas de comedor pueden combinarse con asientos cómodos y descansa brazos anchos.

En bord de mer, on peut prendre ses distances vis-à-vis du design contemporain et choisir un mobilier réconciliant le confort et la tradition. Ainsi, les fauteuils au dossier en bois sculpté selon la tradition peuvent très bien être pourvus de larges bras et de sièges confortables.

Bei der Möblierung eines Hauses am Strand kann von modernen Designs abgeschweift werden und es liegt eine Fusion von Tradition und Komfort nahe. Die ästhetischen, reliefartigen Arbeiten auf den Rückenlehnen von Esszimmerstühlen, sollten mit bequemen Sitzen und breiten Armlehnen kombiniert werden.

The combination between a table made from solid wood and chairs made from woven natural fibers creates a sharp contrast in terms of color and texture.

Una mesa de madera sólida con sillas realizadas en fibras naturales tejidas crea una aguda diferencia en colores y texturas.

Si vous avez une table en bois, entourezla de chaises en fibre naturelle tressée, vous obtiendrez ainsi un contraste de couleur et de textures particulièrement agréable à l'oeil.

Die Mischung eines Tisches aus massivem Holz mit Stühlen aus gewebten Naturfasten, führt zu einem krassen Unterschied im Hinblick auf Farben und Texturen.

Some materials become more attractive when combined with others. Wicker, wood and glass each have their very own textures, colors and qualities that are enhanced when combined.

Algunos materiales ejercen un poder de atracción que se incrementa al combinarse con otros. El mimbre, la madera y el vidrio poseen individualmente texturas, colores y calidades únicas que se refuerzan al mezclarse.

La combinaison de certains matériaux permet de démultiplier le pouvoir de séduction de chacun d'entre eux. Ainsi, en mettant en présence des matériaux possédant chacun leurs qualités de texture, de couleur et de chaleur comme l'osier, le bois et le verre, vous en rehausserez les effets.

Einige Materialien wirken besonders attraktiv, wenn sie mit anderen Materialien kombiniert werden. Korbgeflecht, Holz und Glas haben einzigartige Texturen, Farben und Qualitäten, die bei Mischung mit anderen Materialien hervorgehoben werden.

The range of backrests currently available, in terms of finishes, designs and materials, means there are many options for decorating the dining room. Vertical and horizontal openings can be as fascinating as the textures of fibers or the softness of textiles.

La variedad de respaldos posibles tanto en acabados como en diseños y materiales significa hoy en día una opción importante para la decoración del comedor. Los calados verticales y horizontales pueden ser tan fascinantes como las texturas de las fibras o la suavidad de los textiles.

Il existe un grand nombre de possibilités en matière de dossiers de chaise, tant au niveau du design, des matériaux que des finitions ; ce choix aura des répercussions sur la décoration de votre salle à manger. Les dossiers ajourés horizontalement ou verticalement sont tout aussi agréables pour les sens que la texture des fibres ou la douceur des textiles.

Die Vielfalt an möglichen Rückenlehnen, sowohl in Bezug auf Oberflächen und Materialien als auch auf das Design, ist heutzutage ein wichtiger Aspekt im Hinblick auf die Dekoration des Esszimmers. Senkrechte und waagerechte Verzierungen können genauso faszinierend sein wie Texturen und Fasern oder die Weichheit der Textilien.

bathrooms
baños
salles de bains
badezimmer

washbasins lavabos lavabos waschbecken

As humble as a washbasin may seem, it is possibly the most flexible item of bathroom furniture in terms of the options it affords for experimenting with different shapes, materials and colors.

Por cotidiano que pueda parecer un lavabo, es posiblemente el objeto que forma parte del mobiliario de baño que más se presta para experimentar con sus formas, materiales y colores.

Aussi banal que puisse paraître un lavabo, c'est probablement le meuble de salle de bains qui existe sous le plus grand nombre de formes, de matériaux et de couleurs.

So alltäglich wie ein Waschbecken auch erscheinen mag, ist es wahrscheinlich das Möbel im Badezimmer, das am geeignetsten zum Experimentieren mit Formen, Materialien und Farben ist.

TODAY'S WASHBASINS, supports and faucets offer a whole range of options for designers. Some prefer slender objects, while others opt for bulky items. Either option is fine, depending on the space available. For instance, a large object made of granite, in the middle of the bathroom, housing the support and the washbasin will make a splendid esthetic contribution, especially as it leaves room for movement around it.

EN LA ACTUALIDAD, tanto el lavabo como el soporte y la grifería representan una oportunidad para el diseñador. Hay quienes prefieren objetos con cuerpos esbeltos y quienes se deciden porque éstos sean voluminosos. Cualquiera de las alternativas es adecuada dependiendo del espacio con el que se cuente. Por ejemplo, un cuerpo masivo de granito, centrado en el espacio, que contenga tanto al soporte como al lavabo seguramente resultará de una alta calidad estética y hará lucir el espacio que queda libre a su alrededor para circular.

ACTUELLEMENT, les designers apportent toute leur attention au lavabo, à la colonne de lavabo et à la robinetterie. Certains préfèrent les objets de forme élancée tandis que d'autres les préfèrent massifs. Tous les choix sont bons à condition d'être adaptés à l'espace disponible. Un caisson en granit, disposé au centre de la salle de bains et servant tout à la fois de support et de lavabo, créera un effet saisissant si vous ménagez suffisamment de place pour qu'on puisse circuler autour.

HEUTE STELLEN sowohl das Waschbecken als auch dessen Unterlage und die Wasserhähne eine Herausforderung für den Designer dar. Manche bevorzugen schlanke Körper und manche entscheiden sich lieber für voluminöse Stücke. Welche Alternative die geeignetste ist, hängt von dem Raum ab, der zur Verfügung steht. So hat zum Beispiel ein massives Objekt aus Granit eine grosse ästhetische Qualität, wenn es sich mitten im Raum befindet und sowohl als Waschtisch dient als auch das Waschbecken umgibt. Dies gilt vor allem wenn darum herum Platz zum freien Bewegen zur Verfügung steht.

There are several options for positioning a washbasin in the bathroom. One of them is to embed it directly into the wall, and another is to place it on a surface either with or without some item of furniture beneath it. In the case of a surface, the washbasin can also be embedded or simply placed on top. Rectangular surfaces are the best option for housing square washbasins. If the washbasin is white, an attractive contrast can be created with dark wood.

Existen varias opciones para resolver la presencia del lavamanos en el baño; se puede empotrar directo a la pared o colocarse sobre una cubierta que tenga en la parte inferior un mueble o bien que carezca de éste. En el caso de elegir una una cubierta, también hay la posibilidad de empotrarlo o de simplemente colocarlo encima. Las cubiertas rectangulares son las más adecuadas para alojar lavabos de forma cuadrangular. Cuando el lavamanos es de color claro, el contraste con una madera oscura generará un buen conjunto.

Il existe plusieurs façons d'installer un lavabo dans une salle de bains ; on peut le fixer au mur ou le poser sur un support ou sur un meuble. Si vous choisissez la console, vous pouvez encore fixer le lavabo au mur ou simplement le poser dessus. Dans une salle de bains, les consoles rectangulaires sont plus pratiques que les autres. Si vous choisissez un lavabo blanc, posez-le sur un meuble en bois foncé, cela créera un contraste agréable à l'œil.

Es stehen verschiedene Möglichkeiten zur Verfügung, wie die Waschbecken im Badezimmer angebracht werden können. Es kann direkt an der Wand befestigt oder in einen Waschtisch eingelassen werden, der im unteren Bereich ein Möbel aufweisen kann. Handelt es sich um einen Waschtisch, kann das Waschbecken darin eingelassen oder einfach darauf befestigt werden. Rechteckige Waschtische sind geeigneter für viereckige Waschbecken. Wenn das Waschbecken weiss ist, so wird bei Verwendung einer dunklen Holzart ein guter Kontrast geschaffen.

Many washbasins in the past were oval in shape. One constant feature of modern design is its quest to revive shapes from the past, and now slim, oval-shaped washbasins, placed on bases made from different materials, have become fashionable.

Tradicionalmente algunos lavamanos eran también llamados ovalines, debido a que su forma original era en óvalo. La tendencia a rescatar formas ha sido una constante en el diseño moderno y ahora se han puesto de moda ovalines delgados que se asientan sobre bases de distintos materiales.

Autrefois, certaines vasques étaient appelées "ovalines" en raison de leur forme ovale. Rechercher l'inspiration dans le passé est une tendance constante dans le monde de design actuel ; ainsi, les délicates vasques ovales posées sur différents types de supports reviennent à la mode.

Früher waren fast alle Waschbecken oval. Im Hinblick auf das moderne Design ist eine starke Tendenz zur Wiederentdeckung der Formen vorhanden. Daher sind schlanke, ovale Waschbecken besonders modern, die auf Unterlagen aus verschiedenen Materialien befestigt werden.

Originality is one of the hallmarks of the present day, and bathroom furniture, especially the washbasin, is no exception. Many materials are now used to make this furniture, ranging from the traditional white porcelain to glass and stainless steel, not to mention modern plastic, copper, colored ceramics, stone and even treated wood. In addition, there is also a range of finishes ranging from rustic to highly polished, along with a whole spectrum of textures.

La originalidad es un signo del tiempo presente y ello no exceptúa al mobiliario de sanitario y en particular al lavabo. Los materiales en que hoy son fabricados estos muebles son múltiples y van desde la convencional porcelana blanca hasta el vidrio y el acero inoxidable, pasando por los modernos plásticos, el cobre, la cerámica colorida, la piedra y hasta la madera tratada. A ello hay que agregarle el tipo de acabados que igual pueden abarcar desde lo más rústico hasta lo más pulido, teniendo en medio toda clase de texturas.

L'originalité est un signe de l'époque contemporaine ; les meubles de salle de bains, et le lavabo en particulier, ne font pas exception à la règle. Les matériaux employés à la fabrication de ces meubles sont très variés : de la porcelaine blanche traditionnelle, en passant par le verre, l'acier inoxydable, le plastique, le cuivre, la céramique de couleur et la pierre, jusqu'au bois spécialement traité. À ce vaste choix s'ajoute encore celui des finitions : du plus rustique au plus brillant, toutes les textures sont à votre disposition.

Die Originalität ist eine Eigenschaft der heutigen Zeit und davon sind auch die Badezimmermöbel nicht ausgenommen, besonders die Waschbecken. Es werden heute viele verschiedene Materialien zur Fertigung von Waschbecken verwendet. Dies reicht von traditionellem, weissen Porzellan bis hin zu Glas und rostfreiem Edelstahl. Auch finden moderne Plastikarten, Kupfer, bunte Keramik, Stein und sogar behandeltes Holz Verwendung. Dann sind da noch die verschiedenen Oberflächen zu berücksichtigen, die auch von sehr rustikal bis hin zu hochglanzpoliert gehen, wobei dazwischen jede Art von Textur denkbar ist.

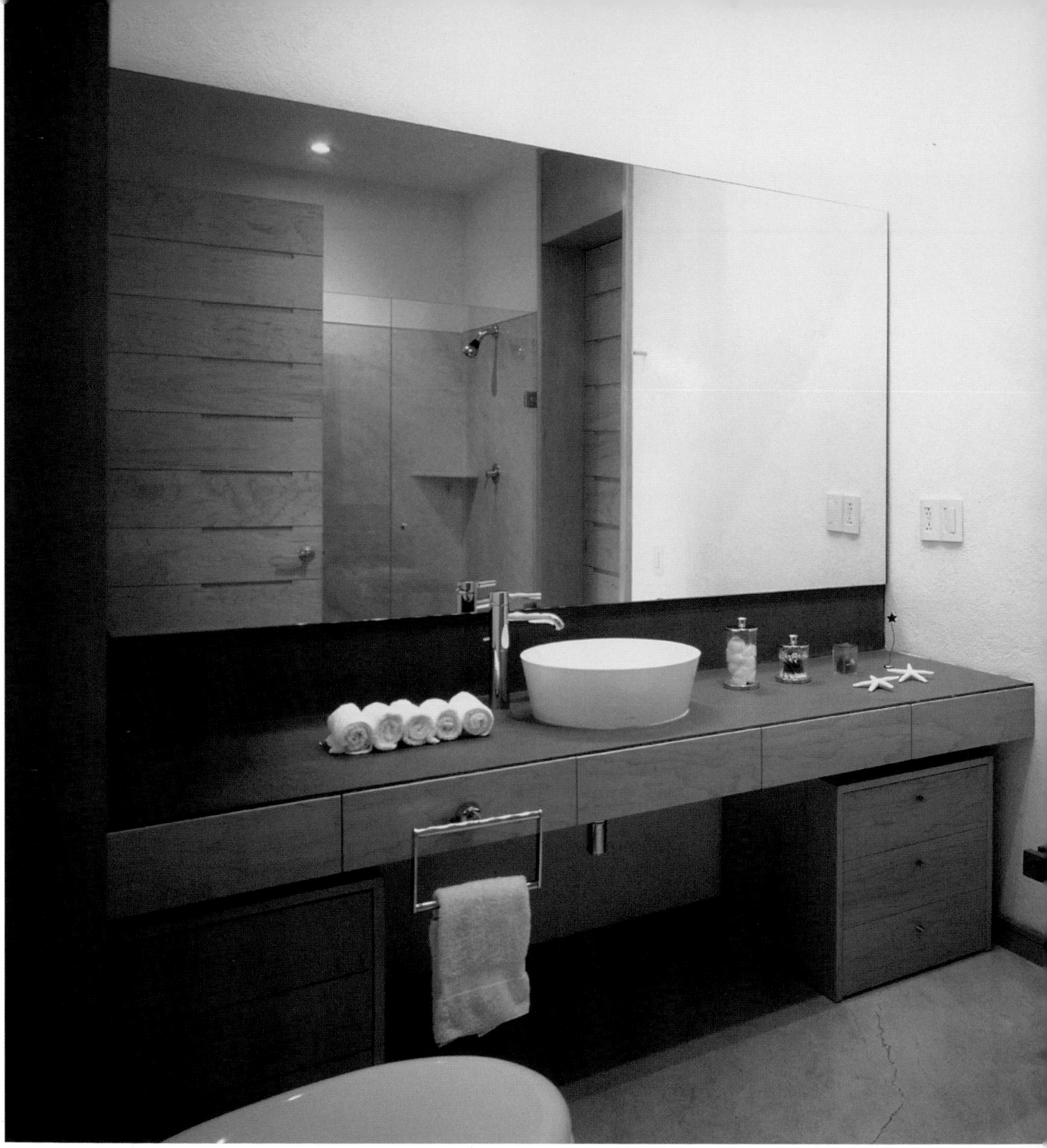

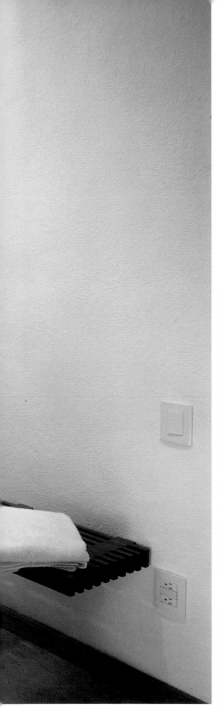

The faucets are an essential component in any bathroom scheme. Many different types are available and the quality is generally good. Many faucets are embedded into the wall while others are, more conventionally, installed next to the washbasin. Some come in a single unit, while others consist of two faucets, and their versatility is as extensive as the imagination.

La grifería es parte esencial del proyecto del baño. La oferta existente es basta y en general buena. Muchos grifos son instalados empotrados a muro y otros de modo tradicional al lado del lavamanos. Los hay monomando o de dos llaves, y tan versátiles como es posible imaginar.

La robinetterie est un élément essentiel dans tout projet de décoration d'une salle de bains. Le marché offre de nombreuses possibilités, généralement de bonne qualité. Les robinets, mitigeurs ou mélangeurs, peuvent être fixés au mur ou disposés sur le lavabo. Au niveau design, vous n'aurez que l'embarras du choix.

Die Wasserhähne sind ein wichtiger Teil des Badezimmers. Das vorhandene Angebot ist gross und im Allgemeinen gut. Einige Wasserhähne werden direkt auf die Wand montiert und andere wie eh und je auf das Waschbecken. Es können Mischbatterien oder zwei unabhängige Knaufe verwendet werden, den Möglichkeiten in diesem Bereich sind keine Grenzen gesetzt.

bathtubs and shower units
tinas y regaderas
baignoires et douches
badewannen und duschen

GLASS is a wonderful option for isolating the toilet and the shower unit from the rest of the bathroom, as well as being hygienic and easy to clean. However, the degree of transparency will depend on how much privacy you want. It is worth looking at several options for using glass for such purposes, including glass treated with acid, as well as opaque or polished glass; these alternatives will allow you to create a translucent but not transparent barrier that will provide the privacy you need.

EL VIDRIO es un excelente material para aislar las zonas destinadas al inodoro y a la regadera del resto del espacio; además de ser aséptico y de fácil limpieza. Sin embargo, de su transparencia depende el grado de privacidad que se consiga. Vale la pena estudiar las diversas alternativas para utilizar vidrios en estas áreas, entre ellas se encuentran los tratados al ácido, los cristales opacos o bien los esmerilados; con estas opciones es factible seguir contando con la sensación de translucidez, mas no de transparencia, y favorecer la privacidad.

LE VERRE est un matériau excellent pour isoler le coin wc et la douche à l'intérieur d'un même espace ; c'est en plus un matériau aseptique et facile à nettoyer. Évidemment, le degré d'isolement dépend de la transparence de la paroi. Les différentes possibilités - verre traité à l'acide, vitres opaques, verre dépoli - méritent d'être étudiées en fonction de deux exigences aussi importantes l'une que l'autre : la luminosité et l'isolement.

GLAS ist ein hervorragendes Material zur Abgrenzung von Bereichen, wie Toilette und Dusche vom übrigen Badezimmer. Es handel sich um ein keimfreies und leicht zu reinigendes Material. Von der Durchsichtigkeit hängt die Privatsphäre ab. Es lohnt sich, die verschiedenen Alternativen im Bereich der Verwendung von Glas zu analysieren. Darunter befinden sich geätztes Glas, mattes Glas oder geschliffenes Glas. Bei diesen Alternativen ist die Lichtdurchlässigkeit gewährleistet, ohne dabei durchsichtig zu sein; dies kommt der Privatsphäre zu Gute.

The platforms into which bathtubs are sunk must be proportional in size to the latter and have enough space for objects such as plants, cushions, ornaments and towels. Their colors should not contrast too much with that of the bathtub, unless you have a very large space.

Las plataformas sobre las que se entierran las tinas deben ser proporcionales al tamaño de éstas y contar con el espacio suficiente para colocar objetos del tipo de plantas, cojines, adornos y hasta las propias toallas. Conviene que sus colores no creen un fuerte contraste con el de la tina, a menos que se cuente con un espacio muy amplio.

Le coffrage d'une baignoire doit être proportionnel à sa taille et avoir des rebords suffisamment larges pour y poser un certain nombre d'objets : plantes, coussins, bibelots et pourquoi pas, serviettes de toilette. Choisir de préférence des couleurs qui se marieront bien avec celle de la baignoire sauf si vous disposez d'une très grande salle de bains.

Die Plattformen, in die die Badewannen eingelassen werden, müssen eine proportionale Grösse aufweisen und auch Platz zum Aufstellen von Pflanzen, Kissen und Dekoration bieten. Auch Platz für Handtücher sollte vorhanden sein. Es ist angebracht, dass der Farbton der Plattformen keinen starken Kontrast zur Farbe der Badewanne bildet, ausser wenn der Raum sehr gross ist.

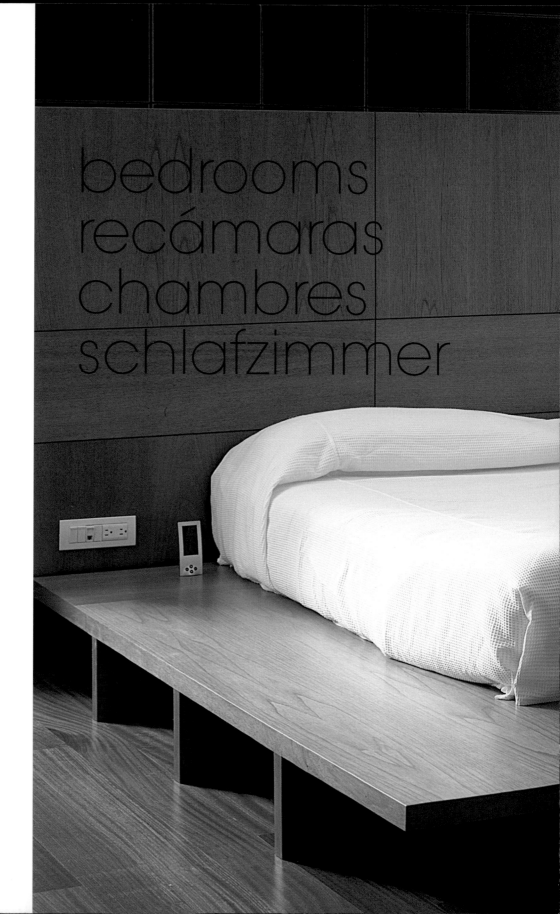

bedrooms
recámaras
chambres
schlafzimmer

THE BED AND THE HEADBOARD without doubt play a vital role in a bedroom. But this is not just because of their size; it is also because they are the natural focal point of this room. The range of options available is as extensive as the spectrum of personal tastes. The current trend, however, emphasizes the use of the color white in the bed linen with virtually no ornaments.

LA CAMA Y SU CABECERA son indudablemente elementos protagónicos en una recámara, pero no solamente por su dimensión, sino también porque son el centro focal natural de esta zona. Las opciones existentes para vestir la cama son tan amplias como los gustos personales. Hoy, sin embargo, invade una tendencia hacia el uso del color blanco en la ropa de cama y prácticamente es nula la presencia de ornamentos en ésta.

LE LIT ET LA TÊTE DE LIT sont sans aucun doute, de par leurs dimensions et de par leur nature, les éléments principaux d'une chambre à coucher et c'est donc sur eux que se porte le regard. En ce qui concerne l'habillage du lit, le choix est tel que chacun peut trouver son bonheur. Précisons toutefois que la tendance à l'heure actuelle est le retour au blanc et aux textiles unis.

beds and headboards
camas y cabeceras
lits et têtes de lit
betten und kopfenden

DAS BETT UND DESSEN KOPFENDE sind ohne Zweifel die wichtigsten Elemente in einem Schlafzimmer, und dies nicht nur aufgrund deren Ausmasse, sondern auch aufgrund der Tatsache, dass sie der natürliche Mittelpunkt dieses Bereiches sind. Die Möglichkeiten im Hinblick auf die Bettbezüge sind genauso vielfältig wie die persönlichen Geschmäcker. Heute geht dennoch die Tendenz zum Gebrauch von weisser Bettwäsche ohne Verzierungen.

WOODEN HEADBOARDS created lengthwise highlight the horizontal dimension of the room and extend the visual plane to the ends. This option tricks the eye into believing that the area is much bigger than it actually is. This effect can be supported by putting rugs on the floor in parallel and making sure the joints of the wood are clearly defined.

LAS CABECERAS DE MADERA que son trabajadas en tablero y de forma longitudinal remarcan la horizontalidad del espacio y extienden la visual hacia los extremos. Con esta alternativa se logra engañar al ojo y hacer sentir que el área es más larga de lo que en realidad es. Para no disminuir el efecto, conviene colocar de modo paralelo tapetes en el piso y procurar que las juntas de la madera hayan sido bien trazadas.

EN CHOISISSANT une tête de lit en bois en forme de long panneau, vous accentuerez le caractère horizontal de l'espace ; le regard sera tout naturellement attiré vers les extrémités du panneau, ce qui donnera l'impression que la pièce est plus large qu'elle ne l'est en réalité. Vous améliorerez encore cet effet en disposant vos tapis de façon parallèle à la tête de lit et en veillant à ce que les jointures du bois soient proprement tracées.

KOPFENDEN AUS HOLZ, die aus einer Platte bestehen und eine längliche Form besitzen, heben die rechteckige Form des Raumes hervor und lassen ihn optisch grösser aussehen. Mit dieser Alternative kann der Eindruck erweckt werden, dass der Bereich länger ist. Um diesen Effekt nicht zu beeinträchtigen, ist es angebracht parallel zum Bett auf den Boden Läufer zu legen. Auch die Fugen des Holzes sollten dieser Richtung folgen.

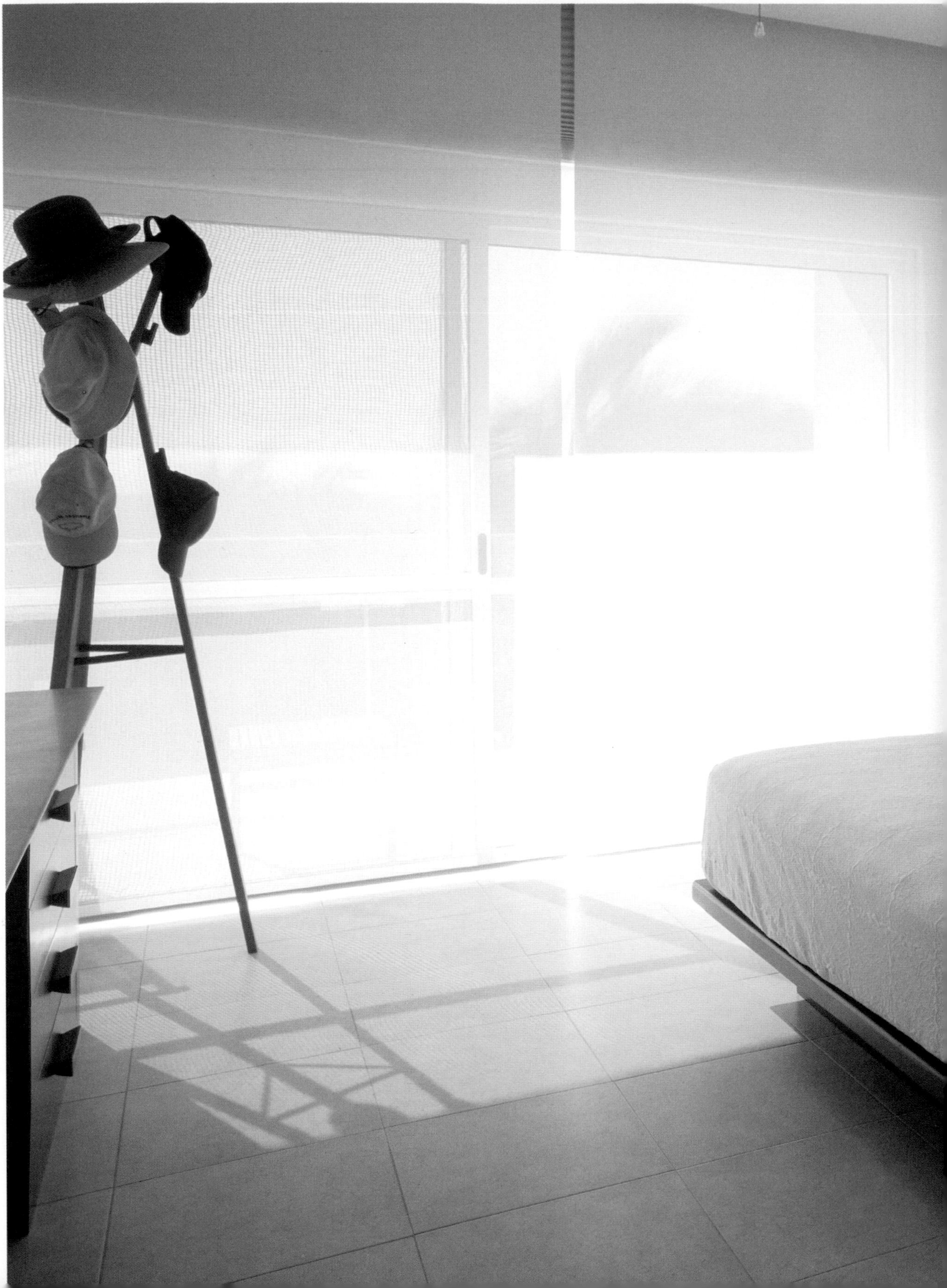

The cushioning and downing of both the headboards and
the bedclothes and pillows are always suggestive of warmth
and comfort, provided by materials that have been expertly
selected to ensure rest and relaxation.

Los acolchados y mullidos tanto en las cabeceras como en
la ropa de cama y cojines ofrecen siempre la sensación de
estar frente a objetos cálidos y confortables, cuyos materiales
fueron pensados con delicadeza y ex profeso para acoger el
descanso y la relajación.

Les effets matelassés ou rembourrés, aussi bien sur la tête de
lit que sur les couvre-lits, couettes et coussins, donneront à
votre chambre un aspect chaleureux et douillet. Choisissez
des matériaux étudiés pour favoriser le repos et la détente.

Gepolsterte Kopfenden oder Tagesdecken und Kissen
erwecken stets den Eindruck von Wärme und Bequemlichkeit.
Die Materialien werden feinfühlig ausgewählt und sind
besonders zum Ausruhen und Erholen geeignet.

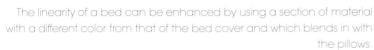

The linearity of a bed can be enhanced by using a section of material with a different color from that of the bed cover and which blends in with the pillows.

La linealidad de una cama se puede destacar a través de un tramo de textil que sea de un color distinto al de la sobrecama y que armonice con los cojines.

Vous pouvez mettre en valeur les lignes pures du lit en posant sur le couvre-lit une bande de tissu d'une couleur différente qui s'harmonisera avec celle de vos coussins.

Die gerade Form eines Bettes kann durch eine Stoffdecke hervorgehoben werden, die eine andere Farbe als die Tagesdecke aufweist und mit den Kissen im Einklang steht.

The human eye is more sensitive to red than to any other color, which is why it is often diluted or toned down with black or white. If black is used, then tones reminiscent of burgundy are obtained, while white produces rosé tones. Burgundy tones are more formal, while rosés are regarded as more casual. Both offer good options in the decorations of a bedroom, such as the main colors and finishes of headboards and bed bases, pillows, some rugs, accessories and parts of the curtains.

El ojo del hombre es más sensible al color rojo que a cualquier otro, por ello, comúnmente se le utiliza diluido y matizado con negro o con blanco. En el primer caso se consiguen gamas de vino, mientras en el segundo se tiende hacia los rosados. Los vinos son formales en tanto que los rosados se consideran tonos más casuales. Ambos son muy adecuados para incluirse en los detalles decorativos de una recámara como son los fondos o remates de cabeceras y pieseras, cojines, algunas tapicerías, accesorios y porciones de cortinajes.

L'œil humain est plus sensible au rouge qu'à toute autre couleur ; c'est pour cette raison qu'on a tendance à le diluer en y ajoutant du noir ou du blanc, dans le premier cas pour obtenir des tons bordeaux et dans le deuxième pour obtenir des tons roses. Le bordeaux apporte une touche de sérieux à la décoration, tandis que le rose crée une ambiance plus décontractée. Quelle que soit votre préférence, utilisez ces couleurs pour apporter une touche finale à votre décoration : têtes de lit, coussins, tapisseries, descentes de lit, accessoires, bordures de rideaux...

Das menschliche Auge reagiert besonders empfindlich auf die rote Farbe. Daher wird dieser Ton meistens mit weiss oder schwarz verdünnt oder abgetönt. Bei Mischung mit schwarz werden weinrote Farbtöne erzielt, während bei Verwendung von weissen Nuancen rosa entsteht. Weinrote Farbtöne wirken formell, rosarote gelten als zwangloser. Beide Farben sind sehr für die Dekoration eines Schlafzimmers geeignet. Sie können für den Bezug oder die Oberfläche der Kopf- und Fussenden, Kissen, einige Polster, Accessoires und Teile der Gardine verwendet werden.

The pale yellow of the wall and headboard that stretches out sideways and includes the bedside tables, when combined with the cream, beige and brown tones of the upholstery and the color of natural fabrics, creates a chromatic sequence that brings warmth to a bedroom and generates a Mediterranean ambience.

El amarillo tenue de un gran-muro cabecera que se extiende en forma longitudinal hasta conformar las mesas laterales, combinado con los cremas, beiges y cafés en tapicerías y con el color de las fibras naturales crean una secuencia cromática que dota de calidez a una recámara y refiere sensorialmente a ambientes del Mediterráneo.

Le jaune pâle d'une paroi faisant office de tête de lit, placée de façon longitudinale pour servir également de table de nuit, s'ajoute aux tons écrus, beiges et marrons des tapisseries et des fibres naturelles pour créer une séquence chromatique chatoyante rappelant la sensualité des décors méditerranéens.

Eine hellgelbe Wand, die auch gleichzeitig das Kopfende des Bettes bildet und sich länglich hinstreckt und seitlich durch Nachttische ergänzt wird, kombiniert mit cremefarbenen, beigen und braunen Kissen sowie mit der Farbe von Naturfasern, schaffen eine chromatische Sequenz, die dem Schlafzimmer Wärme verleiht. Ausserdem wird der Eindruck erweckt, dass es sich um eine Mittelmeeratmosphäre handelt.

By combining the pale wooden tones of the floor, furniture, rugs and walls with the translucent white of the duvets, rugs and curtains, we can create a sensation of increased spaciousness and, above all, a very clean, serene and bright ambience. This is why the abundance, weight and hang of the textiles are essential to enhance the effect in these cases.

Cuando las tonalidades claras de la madera de los pisos y los muebles, de los tapetes y los muros, se mezclan con el blanco diáfano de edredones, tapices y cortinajes se consiguen espacios que dan la impresión de ser de mayor dimensión del que realmente tienen pero, sobre todo, se logran atmósferas muy nítidas, serenas y luminosas. Es por ello que en estos casos, la abundancia, el peso y la caída de los textiles es esencial para hacer mayúsculo el efecto.

Quand les tonalités claires du parquet, des meubles en bois, des tissus et des murs se marient avec le blanc diaphane des édredons, des tapis et des rideaux, l'espace paraît non seulement plus grand qu'il ne l'est en réalité, mais aussi plus net, plus lumineux et plus propice à la détente et à la sérénité. Le poids, l'opulence et la tombée des textiles jouent un rôle essentiel dans la définition d'une telle atmosphère.

Wenn die hellen Farbtöne des Holzes der Fussböden und der Möbel, der Teppiche und Wände mit weissen Bettdecken, Polstern und Gardinen kombiniert werden, so wirken die Räume grösser als sie tatsächlich sind. Vor allem wird aber auch eine sehr reine, ruhige und helle Atmosphäre geschaffen. Daher ist in diesen Fällen die Fülle, das Gewicht und der Fall der Textilien ausschlaggebend für einen gewaltigen Effekt.

terraces
terrazas
terrasses
terrassen

tables and chairs
mesas y sillas
tables et chaises
tische und stühle

THE TERRACE is one of the most sought-after spaces among the residents of big cities. How it is used depends largely on personal preferences, weather conditions and even the type of scenery surrounding it. But if one common element is shared by all terraces, it is the need to use the right materials for contact with the great outdoors, including the architectural materials and the furniture.

LA TERRAZA es seguramente uno de los espacios más ambicionados por las comunidades acostumbradas a habitar en las urbes. El acondicionamiento de este sitio depende mucho de los intereses personales, del clima del lugar y aún del tipo de paisaje en donde se encuentre. Sin embargo, hay algo común a estos lugares, y es que los materiales que se utilicen deben de ser apropiados para estar en contacto con el exterior, incluyendo los de la arquitectura y los del mobiliario.

C'EST LE RÊVE de tout citadin d'avoir une terrasse. L'aménagement de cet espace dépend beaucoup des goûts personnels de chacun mais aussi du climat et du type de paysage environnant. Les terrasses et les balcons peuvent être très différents les uns des autres mais leur décoration repose sur un point commun : les matériaux de construction tout comme ceux du mobilier doivent être choisis pour pouvoir supporter les conditions extérieures.

DIE TERRASSE ist sicherlich einer der Bereiche, der durch Personen, die es gewohnt sind in der Grossstadt zu leben, am meisten geschätzt wird. Die Gestaltung dieses Ortes hängt in erster Linie von den persönlichen Interessen, dem Klima und der Art von Landschaft ab, die die Terrasse umgibt. Dennoch gibt es einen Aspekt, der immer zu berücksichtigen ist: die verwendeten Materialien müssen für den Kontakt mit der Aussenwelt geeignet sein, und dies gilt auch für die Architektur und die Möbel.

Dining furniture for the terrace must be weatherproof. Its design can equally contrast with the setting or blend in with it through the use of locally available materials. In the latter case, in a tropical location, the tough and semi-tough natural fibers for seats and seat rests, local timber for table bases and tops, and the use of palm trees to shelter the space may be the perfect option.

El diseño de muebles de comedor para terraza puede francamente contrastar con el entorno o mantener un diálogo con éste a través del uso de materiales de la región. En este último caso, si se trata de sitios tropicales, las fibras naturales duras y semi-duras para los asientos y respaldos de las sillas, las maderas locales para las bases y superficies de las mesas, así como el uso de palmas para crear elementos arquitectónicos que cobijen el espacio, pueden resultar ideales y mimetizar al espacio con el entorno natural..

Les meubles de jardin qu'on utilisera sur une terrasse doivent avant tout pouvoir résister aux intempéries. Au niveau design, ces meubles peuvent être franchement en rupture avec l'environnement ou au contraire en harmonie avec celui-ci, tout dépend des matériaux choisis. Si vous êtes partisan de l'unité esthétique, choisissez des matériaux naturels originaires de la région. Ainsi, si vous habitez une région tropicale, les dossiers ou les sièges en fibres naturelles rigides ou semi-rigides ainsi que les tables en bois de la région et les toitures en feuilles de palmiers constituent la solution idéale.

Gartentische und -stühle für die Terrasse müssen den Bedingungen im Freien widerstehen können. Das Design kann mit der Umwelt im Kontrast stehen oder mit ihr harmonieren, wobei Materialien der entsprechenden Region verwendet werden können. Im letzteren Falle können an tropischen Standorten harte und weichere Naturfasern für die Sitzflächen und Rückenlehnen der Stühle sowie örtliche Hölzer für den Tischunterbau und die Tischplatte verwendet werden. Palmwedel sind zur Abgrenzung des Bereiches geeignet.

The creation of a modern ambience suggests linear designs; however, if cold materials such glass and warmer ones like natural fibers meet in the furniture, the effect achieved could equally be reminiscent of tradition or of modernity.

La definición de una atmósfera de estilo moderno conlleva a pensar diseños lineales; sin embargo, cuando en el mobiliario se combinan materiales fríos como el vidrio y cálidos como las fibras naturales, se consigue un ambiente que igual evoca la tradición que la modernidad.

Si vous aimez le style contemporain, vous serez plutôt portés sur les meubles aux lignes épurées. N'oubliez pas que le mélange des matériaux froids comme le verre et des matériaux chauds comme la fibre naturelle vous permettra d'obtenir une ambiance à la fois moderne et traditionnelle.

Eine moderne Atmosphäre steht immer mit geradem Design in Verbindung. Werden die Möbel aber mit kalten Materialien, wie Glas oder warmen Matarialien, wie Naturfasern kombiniert, wird eine Atmosphäre erzielt, die weder traditionell noch modern ist.

The different types of treated tough woods for harsh weather, such as teak, wenge, Brazilian teak or walnut, are without doubt the best option for terrace dining furniture; in addition to being weatherproof, they create a particularly warm sensation. Nonetheless the overlook effect depends greatly on the finishes of the wood. Boards, drawings, haut and bas relieves can be used, or you can simply bring out the natural grain as a basic part of the decoration.

Los tipos de maderas duras tratadas para intemperie, como es el caso de la teka, el wenge, el cumaru o el tzalam, son, sin lugar a dudas, los materiales más nobles para utilizar en comedores de terraza; pues, además de ser resistentes al medio ambiente, ofrecen un aspecto de calidez único. No obstante, del acabado de la madera depende mucho el aspecto estético. Es posible utilizar tablones, dibujos, alto y bajo relieves, o simplemente optar por exaltar el veteado natural como elemento fundamental de la decoración.

Les bois durs traités pour supporter les intempéries comme le tek, le panga panga, le cumaru ou le tzalam sont sans aucun doute les matériaux les plus nobles que vous puissiez employer sur une terrasse. Outre leur résistance, ces bois ont un aspect chatoyant incomparable. Cela dit, l'aspect esthétique de l'ensemble dépendra beaucoup du type de finition choisi. Vous avez ainsi le choix entre des meubles en bois massif, des meubles sculptés ou ornés de bas-reliefs ou encore des meubles à peine vernis de manière à laisser transparaître la moirure naturelle du bois.

Harte, behandelte Holzarten, wie Teka, Wenge, Cumaru oder Tzalam, sind zweifellos die geeignetsten Materialien für den Gebrauch im Freien. Ausser ihrer Widerstandsfähigkeit gegen Klimaeinflüsse, bieten sie einen einzigartigen Eindruck von Wärme. Der ästhetische Aspekt hängt aber in erster Linie von der Oberflächenbehandlung des Holzes ab. Es können Holzplatten mit hohem oder tiefem Relief verwendet werden. Eine andere Möglichkeit ist die Betonung der natürlichen Maserung als grundlegendes Element der Dekoration.

The choice of whether to use a round table or a straight-edged one is a matter of personal taste, but it also depends on practical aspects such as seating capacity. Round and oval tables have no unusable angles and cater for a greater number of people, ideal for a get-together, while rectangular and square ones, even when rationally designed, seat fewer people and are not very comfortable for whoever gets the corner. In either case, the type of base used is essential for the comfort and look of the table.

La decisión en cuanto a utilizar una mesa redonda o una de ángulos rectos tiene que ver, por supuesto, con las preferencias personales, pero también con aspectos prácticos tales como la capacidad para el número de comensales. Las mesas redondas y ovaladas no tienen ángulos, desaprovechados y rinden para un mayor número de gente y cooperan a fomentar la convivencia; en tanto que las rectangulares y cuadradas, aún cuando presenten un diseño racional, pierden cupo o, en todo caso, no resultan tan confortables para quienes tienen que enfrentar los ángulos. Desde luego, el tipo de base de la mesa en ambos casos es fundamental para la comodidad y la estética.

Le choix entre une table ronde ou une table rectangulaire ou carrée dépend bien entendu de vos goûts personnels mais aussi de certains aspects pratiques tels que le nombre de convives que vous comptez recevoir. Les tables rondes ou ovales offrent l'avantage de pouvoir accueillir plus de monde et de favoriser la conversation ; les tables rectangulaires ou carrées n'ont pas la même capacité, même quand elles sont bien conçues ; elles peuvent être même inconfortables pour ceux assis à un coin de table. Quel que soit votre choix, n'oubliez pas que le support ou les pieds joueront un rôle fondamental au niveau du confort et de l'esthétique.

Die Entscheidung, einen runden oder eine eckigen Tisch zu verwenden hängt natürlich mit den persönlichen Vorlieben zusammen, aber auch mit praktischen Aspekten, wie der Anzahl der möglichen Tischgäste. Runde oder ovale Tische haben keine ungenutzten Ecken und ermöglichen die Unterbringung von mehr Personen, was das Zusammensein fördert. Rechteckige oder quadratische Tische bieten auch bei rationalem Design weniger Platz und sind auf jeden Fall nicht so bequem für diejenigen, die an den Ecken sitzen. Und natürlich ist der Tischunterbau in beiden Fällen ausschlaggeben für die Bequemlichkeit und die Ästhetik.

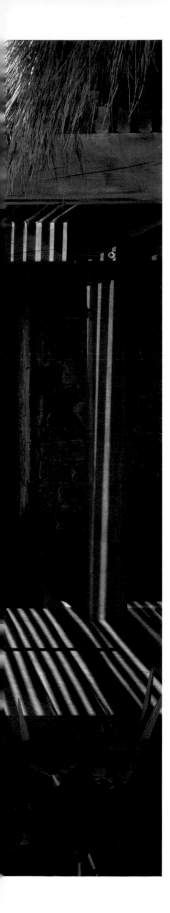

The combination of materials, such as stone or wood for the table, and textiles for seats and armchairs, is an appealing option. The famous director's seats are a great alternative, as the cover can be washed or changed regularly to afford versatility to the decoration.

La mezcla de materiales como piedra o madera para la mesa y textiles para las sillas y sillones es atractiva. Las famosas sillas de director son una alternativa ideal, ya que permiten que la loneta sea lavada o cambiada regularmente para dar versatilidad a la decoración.

Si vous avez une table en pierre ou en bois, il peut être intéressant de l'entourer de chaises et de fauteuils en tissu. Les chaises pliantes ou chaises de réalisateur sont idéales : vous pouvez laver et remplacer le dossier et le siège aussi souvent que nécessaire.

Sehr attraktiv ist ein Materialmix aus Stein und Holz für den Tisch sowie Stoffe für die Stühle und Sessel. Die berühmten Regisseurstühle sind eine ideale Alternative, denn der Stoffbezug kann gewaschen oder ausgewechselt werden, was der Vielfältigkeit der Dekoration zu Gute kommt.

Loose cushions are a great option for the seats of chairs; if they are made from fresh-looking cotton and combined with wood tones, then the textures of both materials will be highlighted. Something similar happens with wicker when combined with materials such as stone on table tops. Another option with a good esthetic contribution are open backrests, which can create a very attractive effect when light passes through them to make shadows and light and shade tones, as well as allowing air to enter hot areas.

Los cojines sueltos son una buena posibilidad para los asientos de las sillas; cuando son realizados en telas de algodón de apariencia fresca, que armoniza con los tonos de la madera, las texturas de ambos materiales lucen al máximo. Algo parecido ocurre con el mimbre cuando se le combina con materiales pétreos en las superficies de las mesas. Una opción más, también con gran valor estético, es recurrir a respaldos calados, los cuales resultan muy atractivos cuando la luz los atraviesa y se producen sombras y claroscuros, además de que permiten el paso del aire, muy conveniente en zonas cálidas.

Les chaises dont on peut retirer le coussin sont particulièrement pratiques. Leurs housses en coton sont fraîches et s'harmonisent parfaitement avec le bois et les deux textures se mettent en valeur l'une l'autre. Vous pouvez obtenir ce genre d'effet en mélangeant l'osier (chaises) et la pierre (table). Les chaises à dossier ajouré sont elles aussi très jolies et très pratiques : s'il fait chaud, le dossier permet à l'air de circuler et aux rayons du soleil de créer de subtiles jeux d'ombre et de lumière.

Lose Kissen sind eine gute Möglichkeit für die Sitzflächen der Stühle. Werden sie mit Baumwollstoffen bezogen, die einen frischen Eindruck erwecken und mit den Farbtönen des Holzes kombinieren, kommen die Texturen beider Materialien voll zur Geltung. Ähnlich gilt dies für Korbgeflecht kombiniert mit Materialien wie Stein auf den Oberflächen der Tische. Eine Alternative mit grossem ästhetischem Wert sind auch durchbrochene Rückenlehnen, die besonders attraktiv aussehen, wenn das Licht durch die Öffnungen scheint und so Schatten erzeugt werden. Ausserdem kann so in warmen Gebieten die Luft durch die Öffnungen wehen.

The tones of the wood used to make terrace and garden furniture vary, but they always provide warmth. If they are exposed to the open air then they will need additional protection from the sun and dampness.

Las maderas de los muebles para terraza y jardín son variadas en tonalidades, pero en todos los casos aportan calidez. Si se les expone al aire libre deben contar con amplia protección para el sol y la humedad.

Le bois, quelle que soit sa tonalité, apportera toujours une touche chatoyante à vos meubles de jardin. N'oubliez pas cependant de le traiter pour qu'il résiste à l'humidité et aux rayons du soleil.

Das Holz, das für die Terrasse und den Garten Verwendung findet, weist verschiedene Tonarten auf. In jedem Fall hat es aber einen warmen Aspekt. Wird das Holz Umwelteinflüssen ausgesetzt, muss es mit einem Schutz gegen Sonne und Feuchtigkeit versehen sein.

MODULAR SOFAS AND ARMCHAIRS are ideal for terraces, as in additional to offering comfort, their upholstery can be removed and washed as often as necessary. The fibers encasing the cushions stop them from losing their shape, although it must be said that the pillows look more modern without the case. Comfort will be further enhanced if we use different ornamental cushions on the armchairs.

LOS SOFÁS Y SILLONES modulares son la alternativa perfecta para las terrazas, pues además de ofrecer confort sus tapices pueden generalmente extraerse y ser lavados con la frecuencia que sea necesario. Los cordones alrededor de los cojines ayudan a que éstos no se deformen, pero es cierto que cuando no los tienen lucen una apariencia más moderna.

El uso de diversos cojines de ornato sobre los de los sillones coopera a una mayor comodidad.

LES CANAPES ET FAUTEUILS modulaires sont parfaits pour équiper une terrasse. En effet, ils sont généralement munis de housses confortables qu'on peut retirer et laver aussi souvent que nécessaire. Les textiles qui recouvrent les coussins les empêchent de se déformer mais donnent un aspect moins moderne aux meubles. Pour plus de confort, n'hésitez pas à rajouter des coussins sur vos fauteuils.

MODULARE SOFAS UND SESSEL stellen eine perfekte Alternative für die Terrasse dar. Ausser einem hohen Komfort bieten sie auch den Vorteil, dass die Bezüge meist abziehbar sind und sooft gewaschen werden können, wie es nötig ist. Verstärkungen an den Rändern helfen dabei, dass die Kissen ihre Form beibehalten, wobei es stimmt, dass sie ohne diese Rundungen moderner aussehen. Der Gebrauch von verschiedenen Zierkissen auf den Sesseln verhilft zu einer grösseren Bequemlichkeit.

sofas and armchairs
sofás y sillones
canapés et fauteuils
sofas und sessel

If the terrace overlooks any noteworthy scenery, then a curved seating arrangement is recommendable. Cushions in thick but fresh cloth and coarse colored casings combine well with furniture made from natural fibers.

Si la terraza se encuentra frente a un paisaje digno de ser admirado es recomendable seleccionar una sala de forma curva. Los cojines tapizados en telas gruesas, pero frescas y de colores crudos, van muy bien si se les acompaña de muebles tejidos en fibras naturales.

Si votre terrasse donne sur un paysage qui mérite le coup d'œil, choisissez un ensemble canapé en forme de demi-cercle. Les coussins recouverts de tissus épais aux couleurs vives vont très bien avec les meubles en fibres naturelles.

Wenn sich die Terrasse in einer Landschaft befindet, die schön anzusehen ist, so sollte die Wohnzimmergarnitur in kurviger Form aufgestellt werden. Die Kissen sollten mit dicken und gleichzeitig frischen Stoffen in Naturfarben bezogen sein. Diese Kombination sieht besonders attraktiv aus, wenn sie mit Möbeln aus gewebten Naturfasern ergänzt wird.

Typical Mexican furniture includes colonial furniture and the so-called "equipales", both of which were used in the old haciendas. Today they can often be found on terraces, especially in a wooded, semi-damp setting. The former is made from light-colored wood, with carved backrests in bas and haut relieves; the latter consists of armchairs and benches with leather seats and supports on structures woven from natural fibers. The artistic value of these items of furniture has won them acclaim in the field of wooden furniture worldwide.

Entre los muebles mexicanos más típicos se encuentran los de estilo colonial y los llamados equipales; ambos se usaron en las antiguas Haciendas y actualmente es común encontrarlos en las terrazas, sobre todo donde el clima es boscoso y semi-húmedo. Los primeros son de maderas claras, con respaldos tallados en bajo y alto relieve; los segundos son sillones y bancos con asientos y apoyos de piel sobre estructuras tejidas de fibra natural. Por el trabajo artesanal que involucran, estas piezas son bien valoradas múndialmente dentro del espectro de muebles rústicos.

Les meubles de style dit "colonial" et les "equipales" sont des pièces traditionnelles du mobilier mexicain. Ils meublaient jadis les grandes haciendas et sont à présent utilisés pour équiper les terrasses. On les emploie particulièrement sous les climats semi humides. Les meubles "coloniaux" sont en bois clair et possèdent des dossiers sculptés en haut et bas-relief. Les "equipales" sont des fauteuils et des bancs en fibre naturelle équipés de dossiers et de sièges en cuir. Ces meubles rustiques sont fabriqués par des artisans dont le travail est reconnu mondialement.

Unter den typischsten mexikanischen Möbeln befinden sich koloniale Möbel und Equipales. Beide wurden früher in den alten Haciendas verwendet und werden derzeit auf Terrassen benutzt, insbesondere dort, wo das Klima halbfeucht ist. Die kolonialen Möbel werden aus hellem Holz hergestellt und haben geschnitzte Rückenlehnen mit hohen und tiefen Reliefs. Equipales sind Sessel und Sofas mit Sitzflächen und Lehnen aus Leder sowie aus Naturfasern geflochtenen Strukturen. Aufgrund der handwerklichen Arbeit werden diese Stücke weltweit im Bereich der rustikalen Möbel geschätzt.

Upholstery with brightly colored lines will help highlight the presence of the sofa in an open space, while plain upholstery creates a sensation of sobriety.

Una tapicería a rayas en colores intensos ayudará a reforzar la presencia del sofá en un espacio abierto, mientras que los tapices lisos cooperarán a dar la sensación de sobriedad.

Les housses rayées de couleurs vives permettent de donner plus de présence à un canapé tandis que les tissus unis et sobres le rendront au contraire plus discret.

Polster mit Streifen und leuchtenden Farben verleihen dem Sofa in einem offenen Raum mehr Aufmerksamkeit. Werden Polster ohne Muster verwendet, sieht dies eher nüchtern aus.

A purged look is best achieved with simple designs and very bright colors. If, in addition, the boundaries between the architecture and the furniture are toned down, the effect obtained will be one of supreme, almost monastic, serenity.

Solamente a través de diseños de líneas simples y colores muy claros es posible conseguir una estética depurada. Si además de ello los límites entre la arquitectura y el mobiliario son diluidos, el efecto que se logra es de una serenidad suprema, casi monacal.

Ce n'est que par les couleurs claires et la simplicité des lignes qu'on peut obtenir un style épuré. Si on parvient de surcroît à effacer les limites entre l'architecture et le mobilier, on obtient une atmosphère de sérénité suprême, quasiment monacale.

Nur durch ein Design mit einfachen Linien und sehr hellen Farben ist eine reine Ästhetik möglich. Wenn ausserdem die Grenzen zwischen Architektur und Mobiliar fliessend sind, kann ein äusserst anmutiger Effekt erzielt werden, der fast klösterlich ist.

The combination of textures, shapes and colors in the terrace furniture enriches the sensations obtained. Some incredible visual and tactile sensations can be obtained from the differences between the softness of cotton and the coarseness of woven wicker or rattan, between the curved and straight contours of the furniture, between the bright oranges and yellows, and the opacity of the browns. If to this we add the colors of the surrounding environment and the contribution of the different decorations, the ambience is a true wonder to behold.

La mezcla de texturas, formas y colores en los juegos sala de una terraza enriquece las sensaciones. Serán extraordinarias a la vista y al tacto las diferencias entre la suavidad de una tela de algodón y la rugosidad del mimbre o del bejuco tejidos, entre las formas curvas y las rectas de los muebles, entre la brillantez de los naranjas y amarillos y la opacidad de los marrones,... Si a ello se le agrega el colorido del ambiente circundante y las tramas de los elementos decorativos, la atmósfera se convierte en algo mágico.

S'agissant du mobilier de jardin, souvenez-vous que le mélange des textures, des formes et des couleurs contribue à enrichir les sensations. Les contrastes entre la douceur du coton et la rugosité de l'osier ou de la liane tissée, entre les formes courbes ou rectilignes des meubles, entre la brillance des oranges et des jaunes et l'aspect opaque des bruns et des marrons provoqueront des sensations extraordinaires… Si on ajoute à tout cela les couleurs du paysage et une décoration bien agencée, on obtient une atmosphère tout simplement magique.

Eine Mischung von Texturen, Formen und Farben in Bezug auf die Couchgarnitur auf der Terrasse bereichert die Eindrücke. Die Unterschiede zwischen der Weichheit eines Baumwollstoffes und der Rauheit von Korbgeflecht oder gewebten Lianen, zwischen kurvigen und geraden Formen der Möbel, zwischen dem Glanz der Farben orange und gelb sowie der Mattheit der Farbe braun, sind aussergewöhnlich anzusehen und anzufühlen. Kommen dann noch die Farben der Umgebung hinzu, wirkt die Atmosphäre magisch.

If the terrace is an extension of the inside of the house, it is a good idea to make sure the two settings blend with each other, by choosing sofas, armchairs and finishes that combine well with those inside the house. Bright woods and colors for the upholstery are good options for the two spaces.

Cuando la terraza es una prolongación del interior es preferible conservar la unidad de diseño entre ambos ambientes, optando por sofás, sillones y acabados que no rompan con lo existente dentro de la casa. Maderas y colores claros en tapicería son buena alternativa para los dos espacios.

Si votre terrasse est un prolongement de l'espace intérieur, il est préférable de garder une certaine unité de style ; choisissez des canapés, des fauteuils et des surfaces qui ne jureront pas avec le mobilier qui se trouve à l'intérieur de la maison. Le bois et les tissus d'ameublement de couleur claire sont une bonne solution pour les deux espaces.

Wenn die Terrasse eine Erweiterung des Innenraumes darstellt, sollte eine Einheit zwischen dem Design beider Bereiche vorhanden sein. Dabei sollten Sofas, Sessel und Materialien gewählt werden, die zu den vorhandenen Möbeln im Inneren des Hauses passen. Helles Holz und helle Polster stellen eine gute Alternative für beide Bereiche dar.

divans
camastros y tumbonas
chaises longues
liegestühle

THE DIVAN in a terrace is the equivalent of the chaise longue in the living room. These items of furniture guarantee comfort and relaxation. They consist of a supporting structure, which may be made of wood, metal, fiber or other materials, with comfortable cushions or small mattresses of varying thicknesses on top wrapped in a range of different textiles, colors and designs.

LA TUMBONA en la terraza tiene como mejor equivalente al chaise longue en una sala. Son muebles para brindar toda la comodidad e invitar al relajamiento. Las tumbonas se componen de una estructura que les da soporte que puede estar hecha de madera, metal, fibra u otro material; sobre ellas reposan cómodos colchones o colchonetas de diversos grosores, que son forrados en la más amplia variedad de textiles, colores y estampados.

LA CHAISE LONGUE disposée sur la terrasse joue le même rôle que la méridienne dans un salon. Ces meubles invitent immédiatement à la détente. Les chaises longues peuvent avoir une structure en bois, en métal, en fibre naturelle ou en tout autre matériau. Il ne reste plus qu'à les équiper de matelas épais ou non, recouverts de housses dont les matériaux de fabrication, les motifs et les coloris peuvent être extrêmement variables.

EINE LIEGE auf der Terrasse ist das ideale Gegenstück zu einem Chaise longue im Wohnzimmer. Es handelt sich um Möbel, die sehr bequem sind und zum Ausruhen einladen. Liegen bestehen aus einer Stützstruktur, die aus Holz, Metall, Fasern oder anderen Materialien bestehen kann. Darauf liegen bequeme Kissen oder Matratzen verschiedener Dicke, die Bezüge mit den unterschiedlichsten Stoffen, Farben und Mustern aufweisen können.

A folding bed can be placed at floor level, either simply bearing in mind ergonomic requirements or raised on legs, with or without wheels. The main thing is that it must be possible to move the headboard to different positions, depending on the varying needs of users.

Un camastro puede estar colocado a ras del suelo siguiendo simplemente formas ergonómicas, o bien en altura sobre patas con ruedas o sin éstas. Lo más importante es que la cabecera se pueda graduar en distintas posiciones, según lo requiera en diferentes momentos quien la use.

On peut disposer une couchette au ras du sol en suivant simplement les formes ergonomiques ou encore l'installer sur des pieds ou sur des roulettes. Le plus important est de la munir d'un dossier réglable pour que chacun puisse s'installer dans sa position favorite.

Ein Liegestuhl kann direkt auf dem Boden angebracht werden und einfachen ergonomischen Formen folgen oder auf Stuhlbeinen mit oder ohne Räder stehen. Der wichtigste Aspekt ist, dass das Kopfende verstellt werden kann, damit der Benutzer in allen Situationen bequem liegt.

Furniture made from natural fibers, such as bamboo, wicker or rattan are the best option for a semi-closed terrace, given that treated wood and metal are more weatherproof.

Los muebles de fibra natural como el bambú, el mimbre o el rattán son más adecuados para una terraza semi-cerrada, en tanto que los de madera tratada y los de metal son mayormente resistentes a la intemperie.

Les meubles en fibres naturelles comme le bambou, l'osier ou le rotin sont parfaits pour équiper une terrasse abritée ; si votre terrasse n'est pas suffisamment protégée, choisissez des meubles en bois traité ou en métal.

Möbel aus Naturfasern, wie Bambus, Korbgeflecht oder Rattan sind die geeignetsten Möbel für eine halboffene Terrasse. Behandeltes Holz und Metalle sind widerstandsfähiger gegen Umwelteinflüsse.

The armrests of sunbathing furniture can be comfortable, but they can also block out sunrays that would otherwise reach the sides.

Los brazos y ante brazos de los muebles para tomar el sol pueden resultar cómodos y, sin embargo, en ocasiones ser una limitante para recibir un baño lateral de sol.

Les bras des chaises longues sont certes très utiles mais peuvent aussi bloquer les rayons du soleil et gêner le bronzage latéral.

Armlehnen an Möbeln zum Sonnen können bequem sein. Dennoch stellen sie in einigen Fällen eine Behinderung beim Sonnenbad der seitlichen Partien dar.

Seat structures with organic shapes are evocative of nature and comfortable, while straight lines are esthetic and functional.

Las estructuras para asientos con formas orgánicas recuerdan a la naturaleza y son cómodas, mientras que las de líneas rectas son estéticas y también funcionales.

Les sièges aux structures végétales rappellent la nature et sont confortables ; ceux dont les lignes sont droites sont très esthétiques, mais aussi fonctionnels.

Sitzstrukturen mit organischen Formen erinnern an die Natur und sind bequem, während gerade Linien ästhetisch und auch zweckmässig sind.

White is the brightest color around and offers the greatest feeling of freshness. Also, it is not decolorized by sunlight. Its neutrality highlights any colors outdoors, but without losing its own brilliance.

El blanco es el color más luminoso que existe y el que mayor sensación de frescura ofrece, además de ser resistente a la decoloración por efecto de la luz del sol. Su neutralidad hace resaltar todos los colores del exterior, sin que por ello pierda su propio fulgor.

Le blanc est la couleur la plus lumineuse et c'est elle qui apporte la plus grande sensation de fraîcheur ; c'est de plus une couleur qui résiste bien aux rayons du soleil. Sa neutralité permet de mettre en valeur toutes les autres couleurs de l'extérieur tout en conservant son propre éclat.

Weiss ist die hellste Farbe die es gibt, die darüber hinaus auch den grössten Eindruck von Frische erweckt. Ferner werden weisse Bezüge nicht durch das Sonnenlicht ausgeblichen. Die Neutralität der Farbe weiss hebt alle anderen Farben in der Umgebung hervor, ohne dass dadurch der eigene Glanz verloren geht.

A folding bed can be as comfortable as an armchair with an adjustable backrest. The two make good options for relaxation and one does not necessarily mean the absence of the other, as they offer the human body different possibilities and benefits.

Un camastro puede resultar un mueble tan confortable como la silla de respaldo móvil. Los dos son siempre una alternativa para el relajamiento y no necesariamente uno implica la sustitución del otro, pues cada uno ofrece distintas posibilidades y ventajas para el cuerpo.

Les couchettes peuvent être tout aussi confortables
que les chaises longues à dossier réglable. Ces deux
meubles invitent à la détente et le choix de l'un n'exclut
pas nécessairement l'autre puisque tous deux ont des
avantages différents et apportent un confort particulier.

Ein Liegestuhl kann genauso bequem wie ein Stuhl mit
beweglicher Rückenlehne sein. Beide stellen immer eine
Alternative zum Ausruhen dar. Und wenn Liegen vorhanden
sind heisst das nicht, dass ausserdem keine Stühle mehr
verwendet werden können, denn jedes Möbel bietet
verschiedene Möglichkeiten und Vorteile für den Körper.

A decorative scheme based on a variety of differently shaped and sized seats and sun beds, along with different types, can be very appealing if the most is made of the space available and the seats, divans and stools are arranged on different levels. The combination of textures will also help highlight the range of the furniture present.

Una decoración con una variedad de formas, tipos y tamaños de asientos y asoleaderos puede ser muy seductora si también se aprovecha el espacio y se disponen las sillas, tumbonas y taburetes en distintos planos. La combinación de texturas ayudará también a resaltar la multiplicidad del mobiliario.

Une décoration reposant sur la variété des formes, des styles et des dimensions des sièges sera toujours attrayante, surtout si on dispose les chaises longues et les tabourets sur différents plans de manière à tirer au mieux parti de l'espace disponible. Le mélange des textures permet de mettre en évidence la diversité du mobilier.

Eine Dekoration mit Stühlen, die verschiedene Formen, Typen und Grössen aufweisen, kann sehr verführrerisch sein. Besonders wenn dabei der Platz genutzt wird und auf den verschiedenen Ebenen sowohl Stühle und Liegen als auch Hocker zum Einsatz kommen. Die Mischung von Texturen hilft auch dabei, die Vielfalt der Möbel hervorzuheben.

The esthetic and functional possibilities of the divans can be infinitely sophisticated and original, and the materials also offer a whole range of options. You can go for a large mattress wrapped in towel cloth or some other type of cotton, or an item of furniture with a headrest and a footrest, or simple stools that are easy to move around.

Las posibilidades estéticas y funcionales de las tumbonas llegan a ser tan sofisticadas y originales como se quiera, así como sus materiales representan un universo de opciones. Es factible optar desde por un gran colchón forrado en tela de toalla o de algún otro tipo de algodón, hasta por un mueble con cabecera y piecera, o bien por simples taburetes a los que se les pueda desplazar con facilidad.

Les chaises longues offrent des possibilités esthétiques et fonctionnelles dont la sophistication et l'originalité peuvent être poussées aussi loin qu'on le souhaite. Les matériaux disponibles constituent également tout un univers : vous pouvez choisir un grand matelas recouvert de tissu-éponge ou de coton ou bien une chaise longue réglable ou encore un ensemble de tabourets et de poufs que vous pourrez déplacer à votre gré.

Die ästhetische und funktionelle Vielfalt an Liegen ist unglaublich gross und originell. Auch im Bereich der Materialien kann aus einer Unzahl an Möglichkeiten ausgewählt werden. Es kann zum Beispiel eine grosse Matratze mit einem Bezug aus Handtuchstoff oder einem anderen Baumwollstoff verwendet werden oder ein Möbel mit Kopf- und Fussende oder gar einfache Hocker, die leicht von einem Ort an den anderen gestellt werden können.

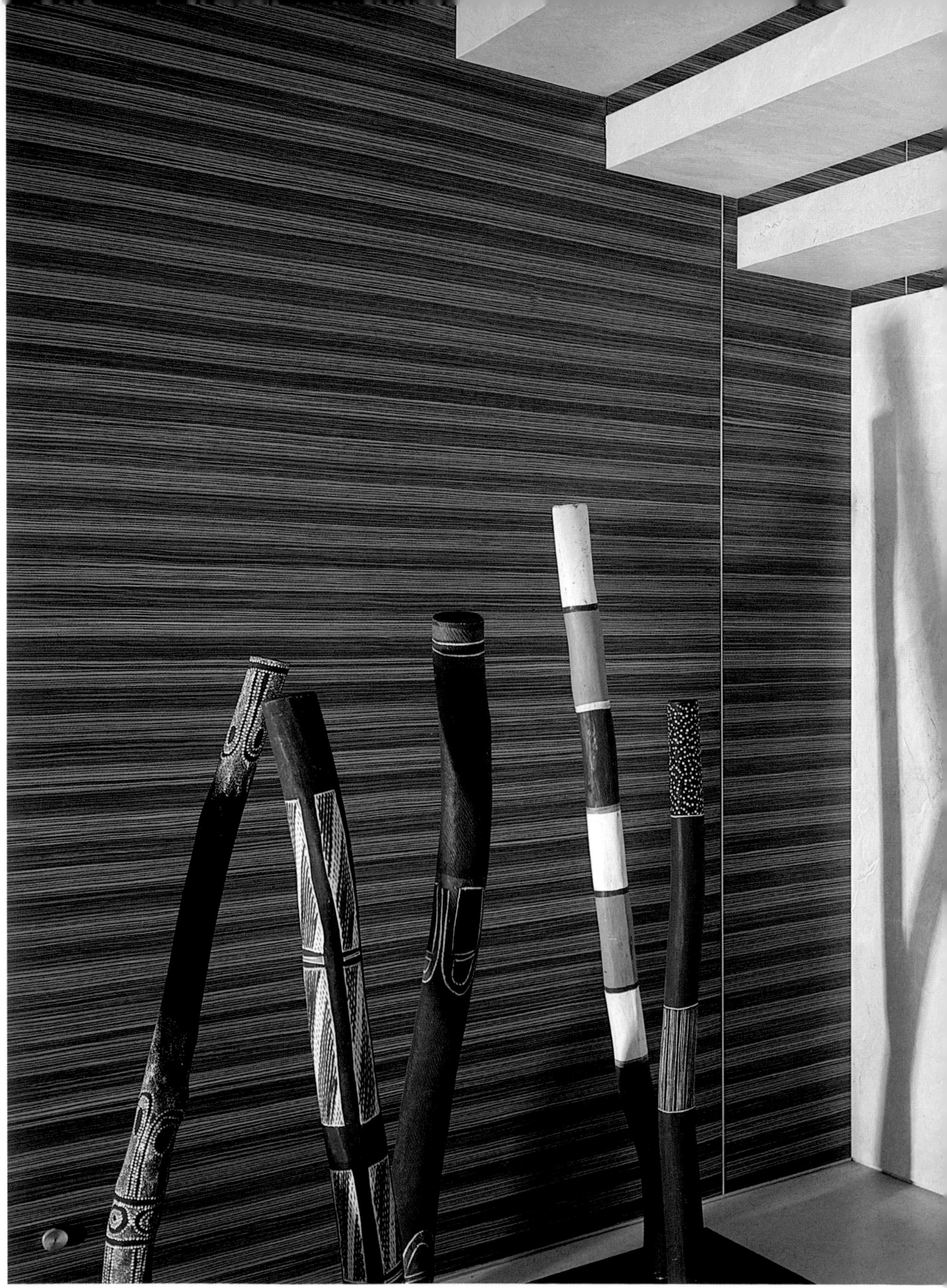

decorative elements
elementos decorativos
éléments décoratifs
dekorative elemente

sculptures
esculturas
sculptures
skulpturen

WHEN PEOPLE TALK ABOUT taking care of detail in a house, they are not just referring to the architectural finishes but also to decorative elements distributed around the home. An attractive item that has been badly positioned can have a disastrous effect on the decoration, as could an object that is simply not right for the place in question. Great care must be taken with sculptures, as they are artistic items that must be well illuminated and regarded as centers of attention.

CUANDO LA GENTE se refiere al cuidado en el detalle dentro de una casa, no solamente alude a los acabados arquitectónicos sino también a los elementos decorativos que se hallan distribuidos en la vivienda. Un lindo objeto mal colocado puede ser catastrófico para la decoración, pero lo mismo puede ocurrir con un elemento que no sea adecuado para el espacio. Las esculturas merecen especial atención, pues son piezas artísticas que deben estar bien iluminadas y ser consideradas como focos de atención.

QUAND NOUS PARLONS de soin du détail en matière de décoration, nous pensons à la fois à l'architecture et aux objets décoratifs qu'elle enserre. Le fait de placer un bel objet au mauvais endroit peut avoir un effet désastreux sur l'ensemble de la décoration ; il en va de même quand nous choisissons un objet inadapté à l'espace dont nous disposons. Nous nous arrêterons sur les sculptures qui, en tant qu'objets d'art, méritent d'attirer sur elles tous les regards ; ce résultat s'obtient à l'aide d'un éclairage approprié.

WENN SICH AUF die Details in einem Haus bezogen wird, dann sind damit nicht nur die architektonischen Elemente gemeint, sondern auch die Dekoration, die im ganzen Haus vorhanden ist. Ein schönes Objekt, das falsch aufgestellt wurde, kann eine Katastrophe für die Dekoration bedeuten. Das gleiche gilt für Objekte, die für den Raum nicht geeignet sind. Skulpturen verdienen besondere Aufmerksamkeit, denn es handelt sich um Kunstwerke, die gut beleuchtet sein sollten und im Mittelpunkt stehen.

Large or medium-sized sculptures must be given enough space to breathe and be admired from different angles and perspectives. If the sculpture's size and presence are imposing and the expressive and plastic loads powerful, a good idea would be to place it in translucent places as neutral as possible, as well as to avoid placing other objects around the sculpture that compete with it or simply pale into the shade next to it.

La escultura figurativa, ya sea de mediano o gran formato, tiene que contar con el espacio suficiente para que la obra respire y pueda ser admirada desde sus diversos ángulos y perspectivas. Cuando su masividad y su materialidad son fuertes y las cargas expresiva y plástica son potentes es conveniente ubicar la pieza en espacios diáfanos y lo más neutros posibles, así como evitar colocar a su alrededor otros objetos que compitan con la escultura o que simplemente se vean minimizados frente a ella.

Une sculpture figurative, qu'elle soit de grande taille ou de taille moyenne, doit être placée dans un espace assez grand pour lui permettre de respirer et pour qu'on puisse l'admirer sous tous ses angles et perspectives. Si vous possédez une œuvre massive et imposante, chargée d'une puissance évocatrice et plastique importante, choisissez un lieu aussi neutre que possible pour l'exposer et veillez à ne pas l'entourer d'autres objets qui pourraient, par comparaison, avoir l'air ridicules ou au contraire lui faire concurrence.

Eine Skulptur mittlerer oder grosser Grösse muss über ausreichenden Platz verfügen, damit das Werk atmen und aus verschiedenen Blickwinkeln und Perspektiven betrachtet werden kann. Wenn die Skulptur und das verwendete Material massiv sind und es sich um ein ausdrucksstarkes Werk handelt, ist es angebracht, das Stück an einen Ort zu stellen, der so neutral wie eben möglich ist. Ausserdem sollte vermieden werden, aussen herum andere Objekte zu disponieren, die mit der Skulptur konkurrieren oder ihr gegenüber nichtssagend aussehen.

The amount of direct light pouring onto the sculpture is a key factor in allowing the viewer to appreciate all its qualities. The lighting will be adequate if it is possible to make out all the volumes, textures and tones of the material, as well as its movement.

El baño de luz directa sobre la obra escultórica es determinante para que se pueda apreciar en todas sus cualidades. Si se distinguen los volúmenes, las texturas, las tonalidades del material y el movimiento, quiere decir que la pieza ha sido adecuadamente iluminada.

Un rai de lumière tombant directement sur la sculpture peut avoir un effet déterminant et permettre à tous de mieux en apprécier les qualités. Un éclairage convenable doit vous permettre de distinguer les volumes, les textures, les couleurs et le mouvement de l'objet.

Ein Bad aus direktem Licht über der Skultpur ist ausschlaggebend dafür, dass all deren Qualitäten zur Geltung kommen. Wenn der gesamte Umfang, die Texturen, Schattierungen des Materials und Bewegungen zu sehen sind bedeutet dies, dass das Stück korrekt beleuchtet ist.

Assigning an exclusive space to the sculpture implies an appreciation of the work of art in question, as well as affording it a scenario on which it can be contemplated. The best option in these cases is to put the object in the middle of the space and let it express itself on its own.

Otorgarle una zona exclusiva a una escultura implica saber apreciar el arte que encierra la obra, pero también darle la posibilidad de ser contemplada. Lo mejor en estos casos es colocar la pieza al centro del espacio y dejarla que exprese por sí sola.

Octroyer un espace spécifique à une sculpture montre que vous en appréciez les qualités et que vous souhaitez qu'elle soit admirée. Le plus simple est de placer la sculpture au centre de l'espace que vous lui aurez réservé et de la laisser s'exprimer par elle-même.

Wird einer Skulptur ein spezieller Platz zugewiesen, so bedeutet dies, dass man die Kunst, die das Werk impliziert, zu schätzen weiss und gleichzeitig die Möglichkeit zum Betrachten gibt. In diesen Fällen sollte das Stück in der Mitte stehen und für sich selbst sprechen.

The predominance of the sculpture depends to a certain degree on who displays it, which means it is essential to bear in mind the finishes in the room that will house it. It is sometimes useful if the materials used to make the walls, floors and ceilings are neutral, although the color of a wall or its finishes may occasionally highlight the full splendor of the sculpture. There are no set recipes for this, but it is necessary to understand what the article requires and then provide it wisely.

El protagonismo del arte en el espacio está de algún modo en poder de quien lo exhibe. Por esta razón, considerar los acabados de la zona en donde se localizará la obra es fundamental. La neutralidad de los materiales de muros, pisos y techos es a veces conveniente, aunque hay ocasiones en que gracias al colorido de un muro o a su acabado es posible que la escultura luzca en todo su esplendor. Si bien no existen recetas al respecto, hay que interpretar lo que pide la propia pieza y resolverlo con talento.

Le pouvoir séducteur d'une œuvre d'art dépend d'une certaine manière de la personne qui choisit de l'exposer. Les finitions de l'espace que vous aurez assigné à votre sculpture joueront un rôle fondamental. La solution la plus évidente est de choisir des murs, des sols et des plafonds aussi neutres que possibles ; néanmoins, il arrive que les finitions ou la couleur d'un mur puissent permettre à la sculpture d'apparaître aux yeux de tous dans toute sa splendeur. Dans ce domaine, il n'existe pas de recette : vous devez être à l'écoute de l'œuvre et avoir confiance en votre talent.

Der Protagonismus eines Kunstwerkes in einem Raum hängt auf gewisse Weise von der Person ab, die es ausstellt. Aus diesem Grunde sollten unbedingt die Oberflächen in Betracht gezogen werden, die sich im Bereich der Ausstellung des Werkes befinden. Wände, Böden und Decken sollten möglichst neutral sein. Manchmal ist aber auch gerade die Farbe der Wand oder deren Oberfläche ausschlaggebend dafür, dass die Skulptur besonders gut zur Geltung kommt. Es gibt keine allgemeingültigen Rezepte, die in diesem Bereich anzuwenden sind. Das Stück selbst ist zu interpretieren und deren Aufstellung sollte mit Talent geschehen.

There are many options for making a sculpture stand out, and the choice will depend largely on how big it is. Some sculptures look better on the floor while others need to be stood on a base of an appropriate size.

Las alternativas para hacer que sobresalga alguna escultura son diversas y la elección depende mucho del tamaño de la pieza. Hay obras que lucen mejor a pie de piso o inclusive enterradas, y otras que es necesario elevarlas con bases que se encuentren en proporción.

Les possibilités pour qu'une sculpture soit mise à son avantage sont diverses et les choix à faire sont pour beaucoup liés aux dimensions de l'œuvre. Certaines seront mieux mises en valeur au niveau du sol, voire même encastrées dans le sol, tandis que d'autres mériteront d'être posées sur un socle.

Es gibt viele Möglichkeiten, die dazu dienen, eine Skulptur besonders hervorzuheben. Die Auswahl hängt entscheidend mit der Grösse des Stückes zusammen. Es gibt Werke, die besser auf dem Boden oder sogar in den Boden eingelassen zur Geltung kommen. Andere Stücke sind auf einen Sockel zu stellen, der proportional dazu passt.

AN UNREMARKABLE OBJECT can become a visual delight if it is well placed or if some change is made to make it look original or simply pronounced. The seductive prowess of objects is closely linked to their sensuality. The bright color of flowers placed in the middle of a dark table, for example, can be as attractive as a couple of conches in a translucent space calmly showing off their shapes and textures.

UN OBJETO TRIVIAL puede convertirse en el favorito para la vista si está adecuadamente ubicado o si se le ha hecho algún arreglo que lo haga ver original o sencillamente resaltar. La seducción de los objetos está estrechamente ligada a su sensualidad. El colorido de unas flores sobre un centro de mesa de tonalidad oscura, por ejemplo, puede ser tan atractivo como observar a dos caracolas que se hallen en un espacio diáfano exhibiendo con placidez sus formas y texturas.

UN OBJET BANAL peut parfaitement être le centre de tous les regards à condition d'être placé là où il le faut ou d'avoir été transformé de manière à paraître plus original et plus agréable à l'œil. La séduction que les objets exercent sur nous est liée à leur sensualité. Un bouquet de fleurs aux couleurs vives posé sur une table foncée peut être aussi beau que deux coquillages disposés dans un espace diaphane, exhibant placidement leurs formes et leurs textures.

EIN TRIVIALES OBJEKT kann sich in das Lieblingsstück verwandeln, wenn es auf geeignete Weise aufgestellt wird, wenn es originell zurechtgemacht wurde oder auf einfache Weise ins Auge sticht. Die Attraktivität der Objekte ist eng mit deren Sinnlichkeit verbunden. Bunte Blumen auf einem dunklen Tisch können zum Beispiel genauso schön sein wie zwei Schnecken, die in einem Raum aufeinandertreffen und mit Sanftmut ihre Formen und Texturen zur Schau stellen.

decorative objects
objetos decorativos
objets décoratifs
dekorative objekte

THE WORKS OF ART that can be admired include wood and stone carvings. Carving provides haut or bas relieves, while polishing will bring out the grain of the material. It is sometimes a good idea to bring together two items with these two alternatives, but care must be taken to avoid overloading the environment, which would deny both articles the space they need.

ENTRE LOS TRABAJOS más admirables en términos artísticos se encuentran las tallas en madera y en piedra. Con la talla se consigue el relieve, alto o bajo, o bien el pulido de una pieza para que luzca su veteado. Confrontar dos piezas en las que se expongan ambas alternativas podría ser una buena idea, pero hay que tener cuidado de no llegar a sobrecargar el ambiente o de correr el riesgo de no darle a cada una el lugar que merece.

LES OBJETS en pierre taillée ou en bois sculpté suscitent généralement l'admiration de tous. La taille permet de créer des reliefs et des bas reliefs tandis que le polissage met en évidence les moirures de la matière. Vous pouvez exposer côte à côte un objet taillé et un objet poli, en veillant toutefois à ne pas surcharger l'espace, ce qui finirait par noyer tous les objets dans une sorte de flou peu artistique.

UNTER DEN ARBEITEN, die als Kunstwerke zu bewundern sind, befinden sich geschnitztes Holz und geformter Stein. Durch die Bearbeitung wird ein hohes oder tiefes Relief erzeugt oder die Maserung wird durch Polieren der Stücke hervorgehoben. Die Gegenüberstellung von zwei Stücken, auf denen beide Alternativen zur Anwendung kommen, kann eine gute Idee sein. Dabei ist darauf zu achten, dass die Atmosphäre nicht überladen wird und jedes Stück den Platz bekommt, der ihm zusteht.

vases and flowerpots floreros y macetas vases et pots de fleurs vasen und blumentöpfe

Plants and flowers with long stalks are ideal for putting in transparent glass vases, but it is advisable to make sure the height of the vases is in proportion to that of the stalks.

Las plantas y flores de tallos largos son perfectas para colocarse en floreros de cristal transparentes, solamente hay que considerar que la altura de los recipientes sea proporcional a la de los tallos.

Les plantes et les fleurs à longue tige sont parfaites pour les grands vases transparents ; pour l'équilibre de l'ensemble, veillez à choisir toujours des récipients de taille appropriée.

Pflanzen und Blumen mit langen Stielen sind perfekt für durchsichtige Glasblumenvasen. Es sollte nur berücksichtigt werden, dass die Höhe des Behälters proportional zur Länge der Stiele ist.

A plant or flower arrangement can acquire the stature of a work of art if put in the right place and in harmony with the surroundings. Tables with organic shapes, such as a mushroom, a flower or something else, may provide the most suitable base for these arrangements. If, in addition, they are put in the middle of the space, in an atmosphere that has not been overloaded, great results can be achieved.

Un arreglo de plantas o de flores puede tener la relevancia de una obra de arte cuando se encuentra en el lugar apropiado y está equilibrado con relación al espacio circundante. Las mesillas de formas orgánicas, ya sea imitando los aspectos formales de una flor, de un hongo o de cualquier otro elemento de la naturaleza, pueden ser más que adecuadas para servir de base a dichos arreglos. Si además se les ubica al centro del espacio, en una atmósfera poco o nada recargada, el resultado es maravilloso.

Un bouquet ou un pot de fleurs peut faire le même effet qu'une œuvre d'art s'il est posé là où il le faut, en respect de l'équilibre de la pièce. Les récipients aux lignes inspirées par la nature, soit en forme de fleur, de champignon, etc., sont parfaits pour accueillir plantes et bouquets. Placés au centre d'un espace net et dégagé, ces bouquets seront du plus bel effet.

Ein Pflanzenarrangement oder ein Blumenstrauss kann die Relevanz eines Kunstwerkes haben, wenn es an einem geeigneten Ort aufgestellt wird und mit der Umgebung im Einklang steht. Organisch geformte Tischchen, die zum Beispiel die Form von Blumen, Pilzen oder anderen Elementen aus der Natur nachahmen, können noch geeigneter als Grundlage zum Ausfestellen dieser Arrangements sein. Wird dieses Tischchen dann auch noch in die Mitte des Raumes gestellt und die Atmosphäre der Umgebung ist wenig oder gar nicht überladen, so ist das Ergebnis wunderschön.

One or several vases made from natural woven fabrics, with or without flowers, can have a powerful esthetic impact, as the very materials they are made from are a testament to their natural origins.

Un florero, o un grupo de ellos realizados en fibras naturales tejidas, ya se que contengan flores o que no cuenten con ellas, podría ser muy efectivo sensorialmente y con su propia materialidad mostrar que su procedencia es también de origen natural.

Les récipients ou groupes de récipients en fibre naturelle, contenant ou non des plantes ou des fleurs, sont particulièrement sensuels car les matériaux dont ils sont faits évoquent immédiatement la nature.

Eine Vase oder mehrere Vasen aus gewebten Naturfasern können Blumen enthalten oder ohne Blumen verwendet werden. Sie sind auf jeden Fall sehr sinnlich, denn das Material selbst zeigt bereits den natürlichen Ursprung.

Many people regard the mirror as a vital decorative element, as it reflects the identity of both the space it is housed in and the person looking at it. It is precisely because of this that it must be strategically positioned.

El espejo es para muchos un elemento crucial dentro de la decoración, ello se debe a que es el objeto que refleja la identidad igual del espacio que lo contiene que de la persona que lo mira. Por ello el lugar que se le dé debe ser estratégico.

Pour nombre d'entre nous, les miroirs jouent un rôle essentiel dans la décoration ; un miroir reflète en effet à la fois l'espace dans lequel il est posé et la personne qui le regarde. Il faut donc choisir soigneusement l'endroit où on va l'accrocher.

Für viele ist ein Spiegel ein wichtiges Element im Rahmen der Dekoration, denn er spiegelt die Identität wider, sowohl der Personen, die sich darin ansehen als auch der Umgebung, in der er sich befindet. Daher ist der Ort für einen Spiegel strategisch auszusuchen.

mirrors espejos miroirs spiegel

architectonic arquitectónicos architectoniques architektonische

48 ezequiel farca y mauricio gómez de tuddo
49 ezequiel farca
50 C'CÚBICA, emilio cabrero, andrea cesarman y marco a. coello
52 ADI / ABAX, gina parlange pizarro / fernando de haro, jesús fernández, omar fuentes y betha figueroa
53 (top) alejandro bernardi gallo y beatriz peschard mijares, (bottom) CC ARQUITECTOS S.A. DE C.V., manuel cervantes céspedes y santiago céspedes morera
54 GRUPO LBC / CHK, alfonso lópez baz y javier calleja / eduardo hernández
55 A5 ARQUITECTURA, alejandro bernardi, gloria cortina, imanol legorreta, beatriz peschard y pablo sepúlveda
56 (top left and bottom) gerardo garcía l., (top right) MARQCÓ, mariangel álvarez c. y covadonga hernández g.
57 MARQCÓ, mariangel álvarez c. y covadonga hernández g.
59 a 61 C-CHIC, olga mussali h. y sara mizrahi e.
62 - 63 ABAX, fernando de haro, jesús fernández, omar fuentes y bertha figueroa
64 - 65 DUPUIS, alejandra prieto de palacios y cecilia prieto de martínez g.
66 a 69 MARQCÓ, mariangel álvarez c. y covadonga hernández g.
70 - 71 TERRÉS / ARTECK, javier valenzuela g., fernando valenzuela g. y guillermo valenzuela g. / francisco guzmán giraud
72 TARME, alex carranza valles y gerardo ruiz díaz
73 MARQCÓ, mariangel álvarez c. y covadonga hernández g.
74 TERRÉS, javier valenzuela g., fernando valenzuela g. y guillermo valenzuela g.

75 gerardo garcía l.
76 - 77 ADI / ABAX, gina parlange pizarro / fernando de haro, jesús fernández, omar fuentes y betha figueroa
78 - 79 TERRÉS, javier valenzuela g., fernando valenzuela g. y guillermo valenzuela g.
80 sixto langarica d.
81 INTER-ARQ, david penjos smeke
82 - 83 juan carlos baumgartner
84 MUSEOTEC, francisco lópez-guerra almada
85 C'CÚBICA, emilio cabrero, andrea cesarman y marco a. coello
86 - 87 FORMA ARQUITECTOS, eduardo ávalos, miguel de llano y josé segués
89 COVILHA, avelino gonzález e., blanca gonzález de o., maribel gonzález de d. y mely gonzález de f.
90 enrique muller y pablo díaz conde
91 DUPUIS, alejandra prieto de palacios y cecilia prieto de martínez g.
92 - 93 ezequiel farca
94 - 95 DUPUIS, alejandra prieto de palacios y cecilia prieto de martínez g.
96 C'CÚBICA, emilio cabrero, andrea cesarman y marco a. coello
98 - 99 DM ARQUITECTOS, javier duarte morales
100 FORMA ARQUITECTOS, eduardo ávalos, miguel de llano y josé segués
101 INTER-ARQ, david penjos smeke
102 COVILHA, blanca gonzález de o., maribel gonzález de d. y claudia goudet de g.
103 A5 ARQUITECTURA, alejandro bernardi, gloria cortina, imanol legorreta, beatriz peschard y pablo sepúlveda

152 MUSEOTEC, francisco lópez-guerra almada
153 CC ARQUITECTOS S.A. DE C.V., manuel cervantes céspedes y santiago céspedes morera
154 - 155 C-CHIC, olga mussali h. y sara mizrahi e.
157 (top) C-CHIC, olga mussali h. y sara mizrahi e., (bottom) MARQCÓ, mariangel álvarez c. y covadonga hernández g.
158 - 159 ADI, gina parlange pizarro
160 - 161 LA CASA DISEÑO DE INTERIORES, jennie g. de ruiz galindo y alejandro fernández d.
162 - 163 manuel mestre
164 - 165 ABAX, fernando de haro, jesús fernández, omar fuentes y bertha figueroa
166 (left) ZOZAYA ARQUITECTOS, enrique zozaya díaz
166 - 167 enrique muller y pablo díaz conde
167 (right) ZOZAYA ARQUITECTOS, enrique zozaya díaz
168 - 169 BR ARQUITECTOS, jaime barba y gerardo ramírez
170 - 171 enrique muller y pablo díaz conde
172 manuel mestre
174 - 175 santiago aspe poniatowski
176 - 177 ezequiel farca y mauricio gómez de tuddo
178 (left) ABAX, fernando de haro, jesús fernández, omar fuentes y bertha figueroa
178 - 179 DUPUIS, alejandra prieto de palacios y cecilia prieto de martínez g.
179 (right) ABAX, fernando de haro, jesús fernández, omar fuentes y bertha figueroa
180 a 182 GRUPO LBC, alfonso lópez baz y javier calleja / antonio artigas
183 alex pössenbacher
184 ECLÉCTICA DISEÑO, mónica hernández sadurni
185 ABAX, fernando de haro, jesús fernández, omar fuentes y bertha figueroa

186 (bottom) GRUPO ARQUITECTÓNICA, genaro nieto i.
186 - 187 (top) TARME, alex carranza valles y gerardo ruiz díaz
187 (bottom) MEMORIA CASTIZA, marco polo hernández y leonor mastretta real
188 - 189 COVILHA, blanca gonzález de o., maribel gonzález de d. y claudia goudet de g.
190 - 191 carlos herrera massieu
192 - 193 ezequiel farca
194 (left) manuel mestre, (right) ZOZAYA ARQUITECTOS, enrique zozaya díaz
195 (left) enrique muller y pablo díaz conde, (right) ZOZAYA ARQUITECTOS, enrique zozaya díaz
196 (bottom) COVILHA, blanca gonzález de o., maribel gonzález de d. y claudia goudet de g.
196 - 197 (top) alex pössenbacher
197 (bottom) ZOZAYA ARQUITECTOS, enrique zozaya díaz
198 sixto langarica d.
199 BH, BROISSIN Y HERNÁNDEZ DE LA GARZA, gerardo broissin y jorge hernández de la garza
200 - 201 ABAX, fernando de haro, jesús fernández, omar fuentes y bertha figueroa
202 (left) DENTRO, javier sordo madaleno, ana paula de haro y claudia lópez-duplan
202 - 203 ABAX, fernando de haro, jesús fernández, omar fuentes y bertha figueroa
203 (right) federico gómez crespo
204 - 205 GA, GRUPO ARQUITECTURA, daniel álvarez
207 (top) C-CHIC, olga mussali h. y sara mizrahi e., (bottom) ABAX, fernando de haro, jesús fernández, omar fuentes y bertha figueroa
208 - 209 ABAX, fernando de haro, jesús fernández, omar fuentes y bertha figueroa

210 manuel mestre
211 carlos herrera massieu
212 - 213 GRUPO LBC, alfonso lópez baz y javier calleja / antonio artigas
214 - 215 ABAX, fernando de haro, jesús fernández, omar fuentes y bertha figueroa
216 (top left and bottom) ABAX, fernando de haro, jesús fernández, omar fuentes y bertha figueroa, (top right) enrique muller y pablo díaz conde
217 enrique muller y pablo díaz conde
218 - 219 ezequiel farca
220 —
221 (top) —, (bottom) ABAX, fernando de haro, jesús fernández, omar fuentes y bertha figueroa
222 - 223 GRUPO DIARQ, gina diez barroso de franklin
224 (top) FORMA ARQUITECTOS, eduardo ávalos, miguel de llano y josé segués, (bottom) ezequiel farca
225 DUPUIS, alejandra prieto de palacios y cecilia prieto de martínez g.
226 - 227 alejandro bernardi gallo y beatriz peschard mijares
228 A5 ARQUITECTURA, alejandro bernardi, gloria cortina, imanol legorreta, beatriz peschard y pablo sepúlveda
230 ARTECK, francisco guzmán giraud
231 GA, GRUPO ARQUITECTURA, daniel álvarez
232 - 233 7XA ARQUITECTURA carlos ortiz y ángel lópez
234 - 235 EL TERCER MURO, ARQUITECTURA E INTERIORISMO S.A. DE C.V, enrique fuertes bojorges y jaime reyes mendiola
236 - 237 MARTOR ARQUITECTOS, enrique martorell y juan ricardo torres landa
237 (right) PML ARQUITECTOS, pablo martínez lanz
238 gilberto l. rodríguez

239 GRUPO LBC / CHK, alfonso lópez baz y javier calleja / edurardo hernández
240 MARQCÓ, mariangel álvarez c. y covadonga hernández g.
241 a 243 gilberto l. rodríguez
244 ALCOCER ARQUITECTOS, guillermo alcocer
245 DUPUIS, alejandra prieto de palacios y cecilia prieto de martínez g.
246 - 247 ARMELLA ARQUITECTOS, mario armella gullete y mario armella maza
248 carlos herrera massieu
249 DUPUIS, alejandra prieto de palacios y cecilia prieto de martínez g.
251 MM ÁLVAREZ INTERIORES, margarita álvarez y juan j. zapata álvarez
252 - 253 C-CHIC, olga mussali h. y sara mizrahi e.
255 FORMA ARQUITECTOS, eduardo ávalos, miguel de llano y josé segués
256 ABAX, fernando de haro, jesús fernández, omar fuentes y bertha figueroa
257 gerardo garcía l.
258 - 259 MARTÍNEZ-SORDO, juan salvador martínez y luis martín sordo
259 (right) MARQCÓ, mariangel álvarez c. y covadonga hernández g.
260 C-CHIC, olga mussali h. y sara mizrahi e.
261 TERRÉS, javier valenzuela g., fernando valenzuela g. y guillermo valenzuela g.
262 - 263 BCO ARQUITECTOS, david gonzález blanco
264 - 265 C-CHIC, olga mussali h. y sara mizrahi e.

photographic   fotográficos   photographiques   fotografische

alberto moreno - pgs. 98 - 99, 105, 114 (bottom right).

alfonso de bejar - pgs. 52 - 53, 76 - 77, 122, 148 - 149, 158 - 159, 184, 244.

andrés cortina - pgs. 160 - 161.

alejandro rodríguez - pgs. 20, 138 - 139, 139 (right), 238, 242 - 243.

arturo zavala haag - pgs. 7 (right). 55, 103 (right), 228.

debora fossas - pg. 133 (bottom), 236-237.

federico de jesús - pgs. 86 - 87, 100, 119 (right), 224 (top).

fernando cordero - pgs. 10 (right), 30 - 31, 45.

guidini - pgs. 80, 198 - 199.

héctor armando herrera - pg. 134.

héctor velasco facio - pgs. 3. 6, 7 (center right), 8 - 9, 11 (left), 14 a 16, 21 (top), 22 - 23, 27, 28 - 29, 32, 36 - 37, 42 - 43, 53 (top), 56 - 57, 66 a 69, 71 (right), 72 - 73, 75, 87, 89, 102 - 103, 106 - 107, 108 - 109, 111 (top), 114 (top right), 115 (top left), 115 (bottom left), 116 - 117, 118, 130 - 131, 146 - 147, 150 - 151, 157 (bottom), 164 - 165, 180 a 183, 185, 186 (bottom), 186 - 187 (top), 188 - 189, 196 (bottom), 200 - 201, 202 - 203, 203 (right), 212 - 213, 214 (bottom), 222-223, 226-227, 230, 240-241, 257.

ignacio urquiza - pgs. 24 - 25, 46 - 47, 64 - 65, 91, 94 - 95, 110 (bottom), 120, 126 (left), 129 (top), 178 - 179, 225. 245. 246 - 247, 249, 256, 258 (left), 259.

joaquín cabeza - pgs. 234-235

jordi farré - pgs. 19, 34 - 35, 35 (right), 44 - 45, 78 - 79.

jorge rodríguez almanza - pg. 237 (right).

jorge taboada - pg. 139 (right), 241.

josé ignacio gonzález manterola - pgs. 178 (left), 179 (right), 207 (bottom), 261 (right).

josefina rodríguez - pg. 141.

luis gordoa - pgs. 18, 53 (bottom), 153.

mario mutschelchner - pg. 138 (left).

mauricio avramow - pgs. 40 - 41, 50, 85, 96.

mayan jinich - pgs. 38 - 39, 59 a 61, 81, 101, 113, 144 - 145, 147 (top), 154 - 155, 157 (top), 207 (top), 252 - 253, 260, 264 - 265.

michael calderwood - pgs. 4 - 5. 7 (center left), 11 (right) 62 - 63, 84, 90 - 91, 110 (top left), 111 (bottom), 115 (top right), 126 - 127. 127 (right), 152, 162 - 163, 166 - 167, 170 a 175, 183 (right), 190 - 191, 194 - 195, 197 (bottom), 208 a 211, 214 - 215 (top), 215 (bottom), 216 - 217, 220 - 221, 248.

miguel garcía - pgs. 136 - 137.

mito covarrubias - pgs. 10 (left). 34 (left), 114 (top left), 118 - 119, 123, 124 -125, 128 - 129, 129 (bottom), 133 (top).

pablo fernández del valle - pgs. 114 (bottom left).

paul czitrom - pgs. 26 - 27, 48 - 49, 92 - 93, 110 (top right), 168 - 169, 176 - 177, 192 - 193, 199 (right), 204 - 205, 218 - 219, 224 (bottom), 255.

pedro luján - pgs. 262-263.

ricardo kischer - pgs. 7 (left). 70 - 71, 74, 142 - 143.

rolando white - pg. 187 (bottom).

santiago barreiro - pgs. 82 - 83.

sebastian saldívar - pgs. 54, 140, 202 (left), 239, 251.

vicente san martin bautista - pg. 130, 232 - 233.

víctor benítez - pgs. 196 - 197 (top).

Se terminó de imprimir en el mes de Enero del 2007 en China. El cuidado de la edición estuvo a cargo de AM Editores S.A. de C.V.